Vegetarian

Everyday Cookery

STAR
FIRE

This is a Starfire book
First published in 2005

05 07 09 08 06

3 5 7 9 10 8 6 4 2

Starfire is part of
The Foundry Creative Media Company Limited
Crabtree Hall, Crabtree Lane, Fulham, London, SW6 6TY

Visit our website: www.star-fire.co.uk

ISBN: 1-84451-307-6

The CIP record for this book is available from the British Library.

Printed in China

ACKNOWLEDGEMENTS

Publisher and Creative Director: Nick Wells
Project Editor and Editorial: Sarah Goulding
Design and Production: Chris Herbert, Mike Spender, Colin Rudderham and Claire Walker

Authors: Catherine Atkinson, Juliet Barker, Gina Steer, Vicki Smallwood,
Carol Tennant, Mari Mererid Williams, Elizabeth Wolf-Cohen and Simone Wright
Editorial: Gina Steer and Karen Fitzpatrick
Photography: Colin Bowling, Paul Forrester and Stephen Brayne
Home Economists and Stylists: Jacqueline Bellefontaine,
Mandy Phipps, Vicki Smallwood and Penny Stephens
Design Team: Helen Courtney, Jennifer Bishop, Lucy Bradbury and Chris Herbert

All props supplied by Barbara Stewart at Surfaces

NOTE
Recipes using uncooked eggs should be avoided by infants,
the elderly, pregnant women and anyone suffering from an illness.

Contents

Baking

Starters & Light Meals

Asian Dishes

Mediterranean Dishes

Hygiene in the Kitchen

It is important to remember that many foods can carry some form of bacteria. In most cases, the worst it will lead to is a bout of food poisoning or gastroenteritis, although for certain people this can be serious. The risk can be reduced or eliminated, however, by good hygiene and proper cooking.

Do not buy food that is past its sell-by date and do not consume food that is past its use-by date. When buying food, use the eyes and nose. If the food looks tired, limp or a bad colour or it has a rank, acrid or simply bad smell, do not buy or eat it under any circumstances.

Take special care when preparing raw meat and fish. A separate chopping board should be used for each, and the knife, board and your hands should be thoroughly washed before handling or preparing any other food.

Regularly clean, defrost and clear out the refrigerator or freezer – it is worth checking the packaging to see exactly how long each product is safe to freeze. Avoid handling food if suffering from an upset stomach as bacteria can be

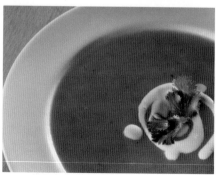

passed on through food preparation.

Dish cloths and tea towels must be washed and changed regularly. Ideally use disposable cloths which should be replaced on a daily basis. More durable cloths should be left to soak in bleach, then washed in the washing machine at a high temperature.

Keep your hands, cooking utensils and food preparation surfaces clean and do not allow pets to climb on to any work surfaces.

Buying

Avoid bulk buying where possible, especially fresh produce such as meat, poultry, fish, fruit and vegetables. Fresh foods lose their nutritional value rapidly, so buying a little at a time minimises loss of nutrients. It also means your fridge won't be so full, which reduces the effectiveness of the refrigeration process.

When buying prepackaged goods such as cans or pots of cream and yogurts, check that the packaging is intact and not damaged or pierced at all. Cans should not be dented, pierced or rusty. Check the sell-by dates even for cans and packets of dry ingredients such as flour and rice. Store fresh foods in the refrigerator as soon as possible – not in the car or the office.

When buying frozen foods, ensure that they are not heavily iced on the outside and that the contents feel completely frozen. Ensure that the frozen foods have been stored in the cabinet at the correct storage level and the temperature is below -18°C/ -0.4°F. Pack in cool bags to transport home and place in the freezer as soon as possible after purchase.

Preparation

Make sure that all work surfaces and utensils are clean and dry. Hygiene should be given priority at all times. Separate chopping boards should be used for raw and cooked

meats, fish and vegetables. Currently, a variety of good quality plastic boards come in various designs and colours. This makes differentiating easier and the plastic has the added hygienic advantage of being washable at high temperatures in the dishwasher. If using the board for fish, first wash in cold water, then in hot to prevent odour. Also remember that knives and utensils should always be thoroughly cleaned after use.

When cooking, be particularly careful to keep cooked and raw food separate to avoid any contamination. It is worth washing all fruits and vegetables regardless of whether they are going to be eaten raw or lightly cooked. This rule should apply even to prewashed herbs and salads.

Do not reheat food more than once. If using a microwave, always check that the food is piping hot all the way through – in theory, the food should reach 70°C/158°F and needs to be cooked at that temperature for at least three minutes to ensure that all bacteria are killed.

All poultry must be thoroughly thawed before using, including chicken and poussin. Remove the food to be thawed from the freezer and place in a shallow dish to contain the juices. Leave the food in the refrigerator until it is completely thawed. A 1.4 kg/3 lb whole chicken will take about 26–30 hours to thaw. To speed up the process, immerse the chicken in cold water, making sure that the water is changed regularly. When the joints can move freely and no ice crystals remain in the cavity, the bird is completely thawed.

Once thawed, remove the wrapper and pat the chicken dry. Place the chicken in a shallow dish, cover lightly and store as close to the base of the refrigerator as possible. The chicken should be cooked as soon as possible. Some foods can be cooked from frozen including many prepacked foods such as soups, sauces, casseroles and breads. Where applicable follow the manufacturers' instructions.

Vegetables and fruits can also be cooked from frozen, but meats and fish should be thawed first. The only time food can be refrozen is when the food has been thoroughly thawed then cooked. Once the food has cooled then it can be frozen again, but it should only be stored for one month.

All poultry and game (except for duck) must be cooked thoroughly. When cooked, the juices will run clear on the thickest part of the bird – the best area to try is usually the thigh. Other meats, like minced meat and pork should be cooked right the way through. Fish should turn opaque, be firm in texture and break easily into large flakes.

When cooking leftovers, make sure they are reheated until piping hot and that any sauce or soup reaches boiling point first.

Storing, Refrigerating and Freezing

Meat, poultry, fish, seafood and dairy products should all be refrigerated. The temperature of the refrigerator should be between 1–5°C/34–41°F while the freezer temperature should not rise above -18°C/-0.4°F.

To ensure the optimum refrigerator and freezer temperature, avoid leaving the door open for long periods of time. Try not to overstock the refrigerator as this reduces the airflow inside and therefore the effectiveness in cooling the food within.

When refrigerating cooked food, allow it to cool down quickly and completely before refrigerating. Hot food will raise the temperature of the refrigerator and possibly affect or spoil other food stored in it.

Food within the refrigerator and freezer should always be covered. Raw and cooked food should be stored in separate parts of the refrigerator. Cooked food should be kept on the top shelves of the refrigerator, while raw meat, poultry and fish should be placed on bottom shelves to avoid

drips and cross-contamination. It is recommended that eggs should be refrigerated in order to maintain their freshness and shelf life.

Take care that frozen foods are not stored in the freezer for too long. Blanched vegetables can be stored for one month; beef, lamb, poultry and pork for six months and unblanched vegetables and fruits in syrup for a year. Oily fish and sausages should be stored for three months. Dairy products can last four to six months, while cakes and pastries should be kept in the freezer for three to six months.

High Risk Foods

Certain foods may carry risks to people who are considered vulnerable such as the elderly, the ill, pregnant women, babies, young infants and those suffering from a recurring illness.

It is advisable to avoid those foods listed below which belong to a higher-risk category.

There is a slight chance that some eggs carry the bacteria salmonella. Cook the eggs until both the yolk and the white are firm to eliminate this risk. Pay particular attention to dishes and products incorporating lightly cooked or raw eggs which should be eliminated from the diet. Hollandaise sauce, mayonnaise, mousses, soufflés and meringues all use raw or lightly cooked eggs, as do custard-based dishes, ice creams and sorbets. These are all considered high-risk foods to the vulnerable groups mentioned above.

Certain meats and poultry also carry the potential risk of salmonella and so should be cooked thoroughly

until the juices run clear and there is no pinkness left. Unpasteurised products such as milk, cheese (especially soft cheese), pâté, meat (both raw and cooked) all have the potential risk of listeria and should be avoided.

When buying seafood, buy from a reputable source which has a high turnover to ensure freshness. Fish should have bright clear eyes, shiny skin and bright pink or red gills. The fish should feel stiff to the touch, with a slight smell of sea air and iodine. The flesh of fish steaks and fillets should be translucent with no signs of discolouration. Molluscs such as scallops, clams and mussels are sold fresh and are still alive. Avoid any that are open or do not close when tapped lightly. In the same way, univalves such as cockles or winkles should withdraw back into their shells when lightly prodded. When choosing cephalopods such as squid and octopus they should have a firm flesh and pleasant sea smell.

As with all fish, whether it is shellfish or seafish, care is required when freezing it. It is imperative to check whether the fish has been frozen before. If it has been frozen, then it should not be frozen again under any circumstances.

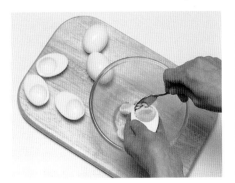

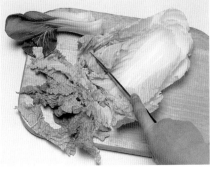

Nutrition The Role of Essential Nutrients

A healthy and well-balanced diet is the body's primary energy source. In children, it constitutes the building blocks for future health as well as providing lots of energy. In adults, it encourages self-healing and regeneration within the body. A well-balanced diet will provide the body with all the essential nutrients it needs. This can be achieved by eating a variety of foods, demonstrated in the pyramid below.

FATS

PROTEINS
milk, yogurt and cheese   meat, fish, poultry, eggs, nuts and pulses

FRUITS AND VEGETABLES

STARCHY CARBOHYDRATES
cereals, potatoes, bread, rice and pasta

FATS

Fats fall into two categories: saturated and unsaturated. It is very important that a healthy balance is achieved within the diet. Fats are an essential part of the diet: they are a source of energy and provide essential fatty acids and fat soluble vitamins. The right balance of fats should boost the body's immunity to infection and keep muscles, nerves and arteries in good condition. Saturated fats are of animal origin and are hard when stored at room temperature. They can be found in dairy produce, meat, eggs, margarines and hard white cooking fat (lard) as well as in manufactured products such as pies, biscuits and cakes. A high intake of saturated fat over many years has been proven to increase heart disease and high blood cholesterol levels and often leads to weight gain. The aim of a healthy diet is to keep the fat content low in the foods that we eat. Lowering the amount of saturated fat that we consume is very important, but this does not mean that it is good to consume lots of other types of fat.

There are two kinds of unsaturated fats: polyunsaturated and monounsaturated. Polyunsaturated fats include safflower, soybean, corn and sesame oils. Within the polyunsaturated group are Omega oils. The Omega-3 oils are of significant interest because they have been found to be particularly beneficial to coronary health and can encourage brain growth and development. Omega-3 oils are derived from oily fish such as salmon, mackerel, herring, pilchards and sardines. It is recommended that we should eat these types of fish at least once a week. However, for those who do not eat fish or who are vegetarians, liver oil supplements are available in most supermarkets and health shops. It is suggested that these supplements should be taken on a daily basis. The most popular oils that are high in monounsaturates are olive oil, sunflower oil and peanut oil. The Mediterranean diet which is based on a diet high in monounsaturated fats is recommended for heart health. Monounsaturated fats are also known to help reduce the levels of cholestrol.

PROTEINS

Composed of amino acids – proteins' building blocks – proteins perform a wide variety of essential functions for the body, including supplying energy and building and repairing tissues. Good sources of proteins for non-meat eaters are eggs, milk, yogurt, cheese, poultry, eggs, nuts and pulses. (See the second level of the pyramid.) Some of these foods, however, contain saturated fats. To strike a nutritional balance, eat generous amounts of vegetable protein foods such as soya, beans, lentils, peas and nuts.

FRUITS AND VEGETABLES

Not only are fruits and vegetables the most visually appealing foods, but they are extremely good for us, providing essential vitamins and minerals essential for growth, repair and protection in the human body. Fruits and vegetables are low in calories and are responsible for regulating the body's metabolic processes and controlling the composition of its fluids and cells.

MINERALS

CALCIUM Important for healthy bones and teeth, nerve transmission, muscle contraction, blood clotting and hormone function. Calcium promotes a healthy heart, improves skin, relieves aching muscles and bones, maintains the correct acid-alkaline balance and reduces menstrual cramps. Good sources are dairy products, small bones of small fish, nuts, pulses, fortified white flours, breads and green leafy vegetables.

CHROMIUM Part of the glucose tolerance factor, chromium balances blood sugar levels, helps to normalise hunger and reduce cravings, improves lifespan, helps protect DNA and is essential for heart function. Good sources are brewer's yeast, wholemeal bread, rye bread, oysters, potatoes, green peppers, butter and parsnips.

IODINE Important for the manufacture of thyroid hormones and for normal development. Good sources of iodine are seafood, seaweed, milk and dairy products.

IRON As a component of haemoglobin, iron carries oxygen around the body. It is vital for normal growth and development. Good sources are liver, corned beef, red meat, fortified breakfast cereals, pulses, green leafy vegetables, egg yolk, cocoa and cocoa products.

MAGNESIUM Important for efficient functioning of metabolic enzymes and development of the skeleton. Magnesium promotes healthy muscles by helping them to relax and is therefore good for PMS. It is also important for heart muscles and the nervous system. Good sources are nuts, green vegetables, meat, cereals, milk and yogurt.

PHOSPHORUS Forms and maintains bones and teeth, builds muscle tissue, helps maintain pH of the body and aids metabolism and energy production. Phosphorus is present in almost all foods.

POTASSIUM Enables nutrients to move into cells while waste products move out; promotes healthy nerves and muscles; maintains fluid balance in the body; helps secretion of insulin for blood sugar control to produce constant energy; relaxes muscles; maintains heart functioning and stimulates gut movement to encourage proper elimination. Good sources are fruit, vegetables, milk and bread.

SELENIUM Antioxidant properties help to protect against free radicals and carcinogens. Selenium reduces inflammation, stimulates the immune system to fight infections, promotes a healthy heart and helps vitamin E's action. It is also required for the male reproductive system and is needed for metabolism. Good sources are tuna, liver, kidney, meat, eggs, cereals, nuts and dairy products.

SODIUM Important in helping to control body fluid and balance, preventing dehydration. Sodium is involved in muscle and nerve function and helps move nutrients into cells. All foods are good sources. Processed, pickled and salted foods are richest in sodium but should be eaten in moderation.

ZINC Important for metabolism and the healing of wounds. It also aids ability to cope with stress, promotes a healthy nervous system and brain especially in the growing foetus, aids bone and teeth formation and is essential for constant energy. Good sources are liver, meat, pulses, whole-grain cereals, nuts and oysters.

VITAMINS

VITAMIN A Important for cell growth and developmemt and for the formation of visual pigments in the eye. Vitamin A comes in two forms: retinol and beta-carotenes. Retinol is found in liver, meat and meat products and whole milk and its products. Beta-carotene is a powerful antioxidant and is found in red and yellow fruits and vegetables such as carrots, mangoes and apricots.

VITAMIN B1 Important in releasing energy from carbohydrate-containing foods. Good sources are yeast and yeast products, bread, fortified breakfast cereals and potatoes.

VITAMIN B2 Important for metabolism of proteins, fats and carbohydrates to produce energy. Good sources are meat, yeast extracts, fortified breakfast cereals and milk and its products.

VITAMIN B3 Required for the metabolism of food into energy production. Good sources are milk and milk products, fortified breakfast cereals, pulses, meat, poultry and eggs.

VITAMIN B5 Important for the metabolism of food and energy production. All foods are good sources but especially fortified breakfast cereals, whole-grain bread and dairy products.

VITAMIN B6 Important for metabolism of protein and fat. Vitamin B6 may also be involved in the regulation of sex hormones. Good sources are liver, fish, pork, soya beans and peanuts.

VITAMIN B12 Important for the production of red blood cells and DNA. It is vital for growth and the nervous system. Good sources are meat, fish, eggs, poultry and milk.

BIOTIN Important for metabolism of fatty acids. Good sources of biotin are liver, kidney, eggs and nuts. Micro-organisms also manufacture this vitamin in the gut.

VITAMIN C Important for healing wounds and the formation of collagen which keeps skin and bones strong. It is an important antioxidant. Good sources are fruits, especially soft summer fruits, and vegetables.

VITAMIN D Important for absorption and handling of calcium to help build bone strength. Good sources are oily fish, eggs, whole milk and milk products, margarine and of course sufficient exposure to sunlight, as vitamin D is made in the skin.

VITAMIN E Important as an antioxidant vitamin helping to protect cell membranes from damage. Good sources are vegetable oils, margarines, seeds, nuts and green vegetables.

FOLIC ACID Critical during pregnancy for the development of the brain and nerves. It is always essential for brain and nerve function and is needed for utilising protein and red blood cell formation. Good sources are whole-grain cereals, fortified breakfast cereals, green leafy vegetables, oranges and liver.

VITAMIN K Important for controlling blood clotting. Good sources are cauliflower, Brussels sprouts, lettuce, cabbage, beans, broccoli, peas, asparagus, potatoes, corn oil, tomatoes and milk.

CARBOHYDRATES

Carbohydrates are an energy source and come in two forms: starch and sugar. Starch carbohydrates are also known as complex carbohydrates and they include all cereals, potatoes, breads, rice and pasta. (See the fourth level of the pyramid). Eating whole-grain varieties of these foods also provides fibre. Diets high in fibre are believed to be beneficial in helping to prevent bowel cancer and can also keep cholesterol down. High-fibre diets are also good for those concerned about weight gain. Fibre is bulky and fills the stomach, therefore reducing hunger pangs. Sugar carbohydrates which are also known as fast release carbohydrates because of the quick fix of energy they give to the body, and include sugar and sugar-sweetened products such as jams and syrups. Milk provides lactose which is a milk sugar and fruits provide fructose which is a fruit sugar.

Guidelines for Different Age Groups

Good food plays such an important role in everyone's life. From infancy through to adulthood, a healthy diet provides the body's foundation and building blocks and teaches children healthy eating habits. Studies have shown that these eating habits stay with us into later life helping us to maintain a healthier lifestyle as adults. This reduces the risk of illness, disease and certain medical problems.

Striking a healthy balance is important and at certain stages in life, this balance may need to be adjusted to help our bodies cope. As babies and children, during pregnancy and in later life, our diet assists us in achieving optimal health. So, how do we go about achieving this?

We know that some foods are advantageous to all, encouraging more efficient brain functioning and better memory. The right foods can also help lower the risk of cancer and heart disease. But are there any other steps we can take to maximise health benefits through our diet?

Babies and young children

Babies should not be given solids until they are at least six months old, then new tastes and textures can be introduced to their diets. Probably the easiest and cheapest way is to adapt the food that the rest of the family eat. Babies under the age of one should be given breast milk or formula milk. From the age of one to two, whole milk should be given and from two to five semi-skimmed milk can be given. From then on, skimmed milk can be introduced if desired.

The first foods for babies under six months should be of a purée-like consistency, which is smooth and fairly liquid, therefore making it easy to swallow. This can be done using an electric blender or hand blender or just by pushing foods through a sieve to remove any lumps. Remember, however, babies still need high levels of milk.

Babies over six months old should still be having puréed food, but the consistency of their diet can be made progressively lumpier. Around the 10 month mark, most babies are able to manage food cut up into small pieces.

So, what food groups do babies and small children need? Like adults, a high proportion of their diet should contain grains such as cereal, pasta, bread and rice. Be careful, however, as babies and small children cannot cope with too much high-fibre foods in their diet.

Fresh fruits and vegetables should be introduced, as well as a balance of dairy and meat proteins and only a small proportion of fats and sweets. Research points out that delaying the introduction of foods which could cause allergies during the first year (such as cow's milk, wheat, eggs, cheese, yogurt and nuts) can significantly reduce the risk of certain food allergies later on in life. (NB: Peanuts should never be given to children under five years old.)

Seek a doctor or health visitor's advice regarding babies and toddlers. Limit sugar in young children's diets as it provides only empty calories. Use less processed sugars (muscovado is very sweet, so the amount used can be reduced) or incorporate less refined alternatives such as dried fruits, dates, rice syrup or honey. (NB: Honey should not be given to infants under one year of age.)

As in a low-fat diet, it is best to eliminate fried foods and avoid adding salt – especially for under one-year-olds and young infants. Instead, introduce herbs and gentle spices to make food appetising. The more varied the tastes that children experience in their formative years, the wider the range of foods they will accept later in life.

Pregnancy

During pregnancy, women are advised to take extra vitamin and mineral supplements. Pregnant women benefit from a healthy balanced diet, rich in fresh fruit and vegetables, and full of essential vitamins and minerals. Oily fish, such as salmon, not only give the body essential fats but also provide high levels of bio-

available calcium.

Certain food groups, however, hold risks during pregnancy. This section gives advice on everyday foods and those that should be avoided.

Cheese

Pregnant women should avoid all soft mould-ripened cheese such as Brie. Also, if pregnant, do not eat cheese such as Parmesan or blue-veined cheese like Stilton as they carry the risk of potential listeria. It is fine for pregnant women to carry on eating hard cheese like Cheddar, as well as cottage cheese.

Eggs

There is a slight chance that some eggs will carry salmonella. Cooking the eggs until both the yolk and white are firm will eliminate this risk. However, particular attention should be paid to dishes and products that incorporate lightly cooked or raw eggs, home-made mayonnaise or similar sauces, mousses, soufflés, meringues, ice cream and sorbets. Commercially produced products, such as

mayonnaise, which are made with pasteurised eggs may be eaten safely. If in doubt, play safe and avoid it.

Ready-made meals and ready-to-eat items

Previously cooked, then chilled meals are now widely available, but those from the chilled counter can contain bacteria. Avoid prepacked salads in dressings and other foods which are sold loose from chilled cabinets. Also do not eat unpasteurised milk and soil-dirty fruits and vegetables as they can cause toxoplasmosis.

Later life

So what about later on in life? As the body gets older, we can help stave off infection and illness through our diet. There is evidence to show that the immune system becomes weaker as we get older, which can increase the risk of suffering from cancer and other illnesses. Maintaining a diet rich in antioxidants, fresh fruits and vegetables, plant oils and, preferably, oily fish is especially beneficial in order to either prevent these illnesses or minimise their effects. As with all age groups, the body benefits from the five-a-day eating plan – try to eat five portions of fruit or vegetables each day. Leafy green vegetables, in particular, are rich in antioxidants. Cabbage, broccoli, Brussels sprouts, cauliflower and kale contain particularly high levels of antioxidants, which lower the risk of cancer.

Foods which are green in colour tend to provide nutrients essential for healthy nerves, muscles and hormones, while foods red in colour protect against cardiovascular disease. Other foods which can also assist in preventing cardiovascular disease and ensuring a healthy heart include vitamins E and C, oily fish and essential fats (such as extra virgin olive oil and garlic). They help lower blood cholesterol levels and clear arteries. A diet high in fresh fruits and

vegetables and low in salt and saturated fats can considerably reduce heart disease.

Other foods have recognised properties. Certain types of mushrooms are known to boost the immune system, while garlic not only boosts the immune system but also protects the body against cancer. Live yogurt, too, has healthy properties as it contains gut-friendly bacteria which help digestion.

Some foods can help to balance the body's hormone levels during the menopause. For example, soya regulates hormone levels. Studies have shown that a regular intake of soya can help to protect the body against breast and prostate cancer.

A balanced, healthy diet, rich in fresh fruits and vegetables, carbohydrates, proteins and essential fats and low in saturates, can help the body protect itself throughout its life. It really is worth spending a little extra time and effort when shopping or even just thinking about what to cook.

Store Cupboard Essentials
Ingredients for a Healthy Lifestyle

With the increasing emphasis on the importance of cooking healthy meals for your family, modern lifestyles are naturally shifting towards lower-fat and cholesterol diets. Low-fat cooking has often been associated with the idea that reducing fat reduces flavour, but this simply is not the case, which is great news for those trying to eat healthily. Thanks to the increasing number of lower-fat ingredients now available in shops, there is no need to compromise on the choice of foods we eat .

The store cupboard is a good place to start when cooking healthy meals. Most of us have fairly limited cooking and preparation time available during the week, and so choose to experiment during weekends. When time is of the essence, or friends arrive unannounced, it is a good idea to have some well thought-out basics in the cupboard, namely foods that are high on flavour whilst still being healthy.

As store cupboard ingredients keep reasonably well, it is worth making a trip to a good speciality grocery shop. Our society's growing interest in recent years with travel and food from around the world has led us to seek out alternative ingredients with which to experiment and incorporate into our cooking. Consequently, supermarket chains have had to broaden their product range and often have a specialist range of imported ingredients from around the world.

If the local grocers or supermarket only carries a limited choice of products, do not despair. The internet now offers freedom to food lovers. There are some fantastic food sites (both local and international) where food can be purchased and delivery arranged online.

When thinking about essentials, think of flavour, something that is going to add to a dish without increasing its fat content. It is worth spending a little bit more money on these products to make flavoursome dishes that will help stop the urge to snack on fatty foods.

Store Cupboard Hints

There are many different types of store cupboard ingredients readily available – including myriad varieties of rice and pasta – which can provide much of the carbohydrate required in our daily diets. Store the ingredients in a cool, dark place and remember to rotate them. The ingredients will be safe to use for six months.

Bulghur wheat A cracked wheat which is often used in tabbouleh. Bulghur wheat is a good source of complex carbohydrate.

Couscous Now available in instant form, couscous just needs to be covered with boiling water then forked. Couscous is a precooked wheat semolina. Traditional couscous needs to be steamed and is available from health food stores. This type of couscous contains more nutrients than the instant variety.

Dried fruit The ready-to-eat variety are particularly good as they are plump, juicy and do not need to be soaked. They are fantastic when puréed into a compote, added to water and heated to make a pie filling and when added to stuffing mixtures. They are also good cooked with meats, rice or couscous.

Flours A useful addition (particularly cornflour) which can be used to

thicken sauces. It is worth mentioning that whole-grain flour should not be stored for too long at room temperature as the fats may turn rancid. While not strictly a flour, cornmeal is a very versatile low-fat ingredient which can be used when making dumplings and gnocchi.

Noodles Also very useful and can accompany any Far Eastern dish. They are low-fat and also available in the wholewheat variety. Rice noodles are available for those who have gluten-free diets and, like pasta noodles, provide slow-release energy to the body.

Pasta It is good to have a mixture of wholewheat and plain pasta as well as a wide variety of flavoured pastas. Whether fresh (it can also be frozen) or dried, pasta is a versatile ingredient with which to provide the body with slow-release energy. It comes in many different sizes and shapes; from the tiny tubettini (which can be added to soups to create a more substantial dish), to penne, fusilli, rigatoni and conchiglie, up to the larger cannelloni and lasagne sheets.

Pot and pearl barley Pot barley is the complete barley grain whereas pearl barley has the outer husk removed. A high cereal diet can help to prevent bowel disorders and diseases.

Pulses A vital ingredient for the store cupboard, pulses are easy to store, have a very high nutritional value and are great when added to soups, casseroles, curries and hot pots. Pulses also act as a thickener, whether flavoured or on their own. They come in two forms; either dried (in which case they generally need to be soaked overnight and then cooked before use – it is important to follow the instructions on the back of the packet), or canned, which is a convenient timesaver because the preparation of dried pulses can take a while. If buying canned pulses, try to buy the variety in water with no added salt or sugar. These simply need to be drained and rinsed before being added to a dish.

Kidney, borlotti, cannellini, butter and flageolet beans, split peas and lentils all make tasty additions to any dish. Baked beans are a favourite with everyone and many shops now stock the organic variety, which have no added salt or sugar but are sweetened with fruit juice instead.

When boiling previously dried pulses, remember that salt should not be added as this will make the skins tough and inedible. Puy lentils are a smaller variety. They often have mottled skins and are particularly good for cooking in slow dishes as they hold their shape and firm texture particularly well.

Rice Basmati and Thai fragrant rice are well suited to Thai and Indian curries, as the fine grains absorb the sauce and their delicate creaminess balances the pungency of the spices. Arborio is only

one type of risotto rice – many are available depending on whether the risotto is meant to accompany meat, fish or vegetable dishes. When cooked, rice swells to create a substantial low-fat dish. Easy-cook American rice, both plain and whole-grain, is great for casseroles and for stuffing meat, fish and vegetables, as it holds its shape and firmness. Pudding rice can be used in a variety of ways to create an irresistible dessert.

Stock Good quality stock is a must in cooking as it provides a good flavour base for many dishes. Many supermarkets now carry a variety of fresh and organic stocks which although need refrigeration, are probably one of the most time- and effort-saving ingredients available. There is also a fairly large range of dried stock, perhaps the best being bouillon, a high-quality form of stock (available in powder or liquid form) which can be added to any dish whether it be a sauce, casserole, pie or soup.

Many people favour meals which can be prepared and cooked in 30–45 minutes, so helpful ingredients which kick-start a sauce are great. A good-quality passata sauce or canned plum tomatoes can act as the foundation for any sauce, as can a good-quality green or red pesto. Other handy store cupboard additions include tapenade, mustard and anchovies. These ingredients have very distinctive tastes and are particularly flavoursome. Roasted red pepper sauce and sundried tomato purée, which tends to be sweeter and more intensely flavoured than regular tomato purée, are also very useful.

Vinegar is another worthwhile store cupboard essential and with so many uses it is worth splashing out on really good quality balsamic and wine vinegars. Herbs and spices are also a must. Using herbs when cooking at home should reduce the temptation to buy ready-made sauces. Often these types of sauces contain large amounts of sugar and additives.

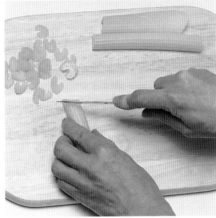

Yeast extract is also a good store cupboard ingredient, which can pep up sauces, soups and casseroles and adds a little substance, particularly to vegetarian dishes.

Eastern flavours offer a lot of scope where low-fat cooking is concerned. Flavourings such as fish sauce, soy sauce, red and green curry paste and Chinese rice wine all offer mouthwatering low-fat flavours to any dish.

For those who are incredibly short on time, or who rarely shop, it is now possible to purchase a selection of readily prepared freshly minced garlic, ginger and chilli. These are available in jars which can be kept in the refrigerator.

As well as these store cupboard additions, many shops and especially supermarkets provide a wide choice of foods. Where possible, invest in the leanest cut of meat and substitute saturated fats such as cream, butter and cheese with low-fat or half-fat alternatives.

Herbs and Spices

Herbs are easy to grow and a garden is not needed as they can easily thrive on a small patio, window box or even on a windowsill. It is worth the effort to plant a few herbs as they do not require much attention or nurturing. The reward will be a range of fresh herbs available whenever needed, and fresh flavours that cannot be beaten to add to any dish that is being prepared.

While fresh herbs should be picked or bought as close as possible to the time of use, freeze-dried and dried herbs and spices will usually keep for around six months.

The best idea is to buy little and often, and to store the herbs in airtight jars in a cool dark cupboard. Fresh herbs tend to have a milder flavour than dried and equate to around one level tablespoon of fresh to one level teaspoon of dried. As a result, quantities used in cooking should be altered accordingly. A variety of herbs and spices and their uses are listed below.

ALLSPICE
The dark allspice berries come whole or ground and have a flavour similar to that of cinnamon, cloves and nutmeg. Although not the same as mixed spices, allspice can be used with pickles, relishes, cakes and milk puddings or whole in meat and fish dishes.

ANISEED
Aniseed comes in whole seeds or ground. It has a strong aroma and flavour and should be used sparingly in baking and salad dressings.

BASIL
Best fresh but also available in dried form, basil can be used raw or cooked. It works well in many dishes but is particularly well suited to tomato-based dishes and sauces, salads and Mediterranean recipes.

BAY LEAVES
Bay leaves are available in fresh or dried form as well as ground. They make up part of a bouquet garni and are particularly delicious when added to meat and poultry dishes, soups, stews, vegetable dishes and stuffing. They also impart a spicy flavour to milk puddings and egg custards.

BOUQUET GARNI
Bouquet garni is a bouquet of fresh herbs tied with a piece of string or in a small piece of muslin. It is used to flavour casseroles, stews and stocks or sauces. The herbs that are normally used are parsley, thyme, and bay leaves.

CARAWAY SEEDS
Caraway seeds have a warm sweet taste and are often used in breads and cakes but are delicious with cabbage dishes and pickles as well.

CAYENNE
Cayenne is the powdered form of a red chilli pepper said to be native to Cayenne. It is similar in appearance to paprika and can be used sparingly to add a fiery kick to many dishes.

CARDAMOM
Cardamom has a distinctive sweet, rich taste and can be bought whole in the pod, in seed form or ground. This sweet aromatic spice is delicious in curries, rice, cakes and biscuits and is great served with rice pudding and fruit.

CHERVIL
Reminiscent of parsley and available either in fresh or dried form, chervil has a faintly sweet, spicy flavour and is particularly good in soups, cheese dishes, stews and with eggs.

CHILLI
Available whole, fresh, dried and in powdered form, red chillies tend to be sweeter in taste than their green counterparts. They are particularly associated with Spanish and Mexican-style cooking and curries, but are also delicious with pickles, dips, sauces and in pizza toppings.

CHIVES
Best used when fresh but also available in dried form, this member of the onion family is ideal for use when a delicate onion flavour is required. Chives are good with eggs, cheese, fish and vegetable dishes. They also work well as a garnish for soups, meat and vegetable dishes.

CINNAMON
Cinnamon comes in the form of reddish-brown sticks of bark from an evergreen tree and has a sweet, pungent aroma. Either whole or ground, cinnamon is delicious in cakes and milk puddings, particularly with apple, and is used in mulled wine and for preserving.

CLOVES
Mainly used whole although also available ground, cloves have a very warm, sweet pungent aroma and can be used to stud roast ham and pork, in mulled wine and punch and when pickling fruit. When ground, they can be used in making mincemeat and in Christmas puddings and biscuits.

CORIANDER
Coriander seeds have an orangey flavour and are available whole or ground. Coriander is particularly delicious (whether whole or roughly ground) in casseroles, curries and as a pickling spice. The leaves are used to flavour spicy aromatic dishes as well as a garnish.

CUMIN
Also available ground or as whole seeds, cumin has a strong, slightly bitter flavour. It is one of the main ingredients in curry powder and compliments many fish, meat and rice dishes.

DILL
Dill leaves are available fresh or dried and have a mild flavour, while the seeds are slightly bitter. Dill is particularly good with salmon, new potatoes and in sauces. The seeds are good in pickles and vegetable dishes.

FENNEL
Whole seeds or ground, fennel has a fragrant, sweet aniseed flavour and is sometimes known as the fish herb because it compliments fish dishes so well.

GINGER
Ginger comes in many forms but primarily as a fresh root and in dried ground form, which can be used in baking, curries, pickles, sauces and Chinese cooking.

LEMON GRASS
Available fresh and dried, with a subtle, aromatic, lemony flavour, lemon grass is essential to Thai cooking. It is also delicious when added to soups, poultry and fish dishes.

MACE
The outer husk of nutmeg has a milder nutmeg flavour and can be used in pickles, cheese dishes, stewed fruits, sauces and hot punch.

MARJORAM
Often dried, marjoram has a sweet slightly spicy flavour, which tastes fantastic when added to stuffing, meat or tomato-based dishes.

MINT
Available fresh or dried, mint has a strong, sweet aroma which is delicious in a sauce or jelly to serve with lamb. It is also great with fresh peas and new potatoes and is an essential ingredient in Pimms.

MUSTARD SEED
These yellow and brown seeds are available whole or ground and are often found in pickles, relishes, cheese dishes, dressings, curries and as an accompaniment to meat.

NUTMEG
The large whole seeds have a warm, sweet taste and compliment custards, milk puddings, cheese dishes, parsnips and creamy soups.

OREGANO
The strongly flavoured dried leaves of oregano are similar to marjoram and are used extensively in Italian and Greek cooking.

PAPRIKA
Paprika often comes in two varieties. One is quite sweet and mild and the other has a slight bite to it. Paprika is made from the fruit of the sweet pepper and is good in meat and poultry dishes as well as a garnish. The rule of buying herbs and spices little and often applies particularly to paprika as unfortunately it does not keep particularly well.

PARSLEY
The stems as well as the leaves of parsley can be used to compliment most savoury dishes as they contain the most flavour. They can also be used as a garnish.

PEPPER
This comes in white and black peppercorns and is best freshly ground. Both add flavour to most dishes, sauces and gravies. Black pepper has a more robust flavour, while white pepper is much more delicate.

POPPY SEEDS
These little, grey-black coloured seeds impart a sweet, nutty flavour when added to biscuits, vegetable dishes, dressings and cheese dishes.

ROSEMARY
Delicious fresh or dried, these small, needle-like leaves have a sweet aroma which is particularly good with lamb, stuffing and vegetables dishes. Also delicious when added to charcoal on the barbecue to give a piquant flavour to meat and corn on the cob.

SAFFRON
Deep orange in colour, saffron is traditionally used in paella, rice and cakes but is also delicious with poultry. Saffron is the most expensive of all spices.

SAGE
Fresh or dried sage leaves have a pungent, slightly bitter taste which is delicious with pork and poultry, sausages, stuffing and with stuffed pasta when tossed in a little butter and fresh sage.

SAVORY
This herb resembles thyme, but has a softer flavour that particularly compliments all types of fish and beans.

SESAME
Sesame seeds have a nutty taste, especially when toasted, and are delicious in baking, on salads, or with far-eastern cooking.

TARRAGON
The fresh or dried leaves of tarragon have a sweet aromatic taste which is particularly good with poultry, seafood, fish, creamy sauces and stuffing.

THYME
Available fresh or dried, thyme has a pungent flavour and is included in bouquet garni. It compliments many meat and poultry dishes and stuffing.

TURMERIC
Turmeric is obtained from the root of a lily from southeast Asia. This root is ground and has a brilliant yellow colour. It has a bitter, peppery flavour and is often combined for use in curry powder and mustard. Also delicious in pickles, relishes and dressings.

Stilton, Tomato & Courgette Quiche

INGREDIENTS

Serves 4

175 g/6 oz bought shortcrust pastry
25 g/1 oz butter
1 onion, peeled and finely chopped
1 courgette, trimmed and sliced
125 g/4 oz Stilton cheese, crumbled
6 cherry tomatoes, halved
2 large eggs, beaten
200 ml tub crème fraîche
salt and freshly ground black pepper

FOOD FACT

Stilton is a very traditional British cheese which often makes an appearance on the cheese board or served with a ploughman's lunch. It gets much of its full pungent flavour, from its veins (created from the steel wires which are inserted into the cheese during the maturing process). It is worth looking for a piece of Stilton with lots of veins that has been matured for longer.

1 Preheat the oven to 190°C/375°F/Gas Mark 5. On a lightly floured surface, roll out the pastry and use to line an 18 cm/7 inch lightly oiled quiche or flan tin, trimming any excess pastry with a knife.

2 Prick the base all over with a fork and bake blind in the preheated oven for 15 minutes. Remove the pastry from the oven and brush with a little of the beaten egg. Return to the oven for a further 5 minutes.

3 Heat the butter in a frying pan and gently fry the onion and courgette for about 4 minutes until soft and starting to brown. Transfer into the pastry case.

4 Sprinkle the Stilton over evenly and top with the halved cherry tomatoes. Beat together the eggs and crème fraîche and season to taste with salt and pepper.

5 Pour the filling into the pastry case and bake in the oven for 35–40 minutes, or until the filling is golden brown and set in the centre. Serve the quiche hot or cold.

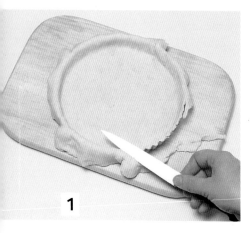

1

3

4

French Onion Tart

INGREDIENTS

Serves 4

Quick flaky pastry:
125 g/4 oz butter
175 g/6 oz plain flour
pinch of salt

For the filling:
2 tbsp olive oil
4 large onions, peeled and thinly sliced
3 tbsp white wine vinegar
2 tbsp muscovado sugar
a little beaten egg or milk
175 g/6 oz Cheddar cheese, grated
salt and freshly ground black pepper

TASTY TIP

For a milder, nutty taste, substitute the Cheddar cheese for Gruyère and grate a little nutmeg over the layer of cheese in step 7.

1. Preheat the oven to 200°C/400°F/Gas Mark 6. Place the butter in the freezer for 30 minutes. Sift the flour and salt into a large bowl. Remove the butter from the freezer and grate using the coarse side of a grater, dipping the butter in the flour every now and again – this makes it easier to grate.

2. Mix the butter into the flour, using a knife, making sure all the butter is coated thoroughly with flour.

3. Add 2 tablespoons of cold water and continue to mix, bringing the mixture together. Use your hands to complete the mixing. Add a little more water if needed to leave a clean bowl. Place the pastry in a polythene bag and chill in the refrigerator for 30 minutes.

4. Heat the oil in a large frying pan, then fry the onions for 10 minutes, stirring occasionally until softened.

5. Stir in the white wine vinegar and sugar. Increase the heat and stir frequently for another 4–5 minutes until the onions turn a deep caramel colour. Cook for another 5 minutes, then reserve to cool.

6. On a lightly floured surface, roll out the pastry to a 35.5 cm/14 inch circle. Wrap over a rolling pin and move the circle on to a baking sheet.

7. Sprinkle half the cheese over the pastry, leaving a 5 cm/2 inch border around the edge, then spoon the caramelised onions over the cheese. Fold the uncovered pastry edges over the edge of the filling to form a rim and brush the rim with beaten egg or milk.

8. Season to taste with salt and pepper. Sprinkle over the remaining Cheddar and bake for 20–25 minutes. Transfer to a large plate and serve immediately.

1

5

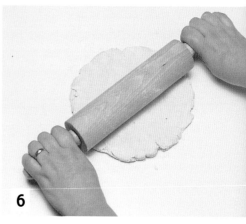

6

Parsnip Tatin

INGREDIENTS

Serves 4

175 g/6 oz bought shortcrust pastry

For the filling:
50 g/2 oz butter
8 small parsnips, peeled and halved
1 tbsp brown sugar
75 ml/3 fl oz apple juice

FOOD FACT

In many parts of Europe parsnips are unpopular. Indeed, in Italy they feed them to the pigs. However, parsnips are great winter warmers especially when mashed with potatoes.

TASTY TIP

This dish is delicious served warm with a Greek salad. Feta cheese is one of the main ingredients in Greek salad and because of its salty taste, it goes particularly well with the creamy flavour of parsnips in this recipe.

1 Preheat the oven to 200°C/400°F/Gas Mark 6. Heat the butter in a 20.5 cm/8 inch frying pan.

2 Add the parsnips, arranging the cut side down with the narrow ends towards the centre.

3 Sprinkle the parsnips with sugar and cook for 15 minutes, turning halfway through until golden.

4 Add the apple juice and bring to the boil. Remove the pan from the heat.

5 On a lightly floured surface, roll the pastry out to a size slightly larger than the frying pan.

6 Position the pastry over the parsnips and press down slightly to enclose the parsnips.

7 Bake in the preheated oven for 20–25 minutes until the parsnips and pastry are golden.

8 Invert a warm serving plate over the pan and carefully turn the pan over to flip the tart on to the plate. Serve immediately.

3

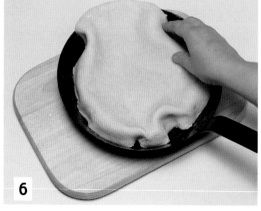
6

8

Fennel & Caramelised Shallot Tartlets

INGREDIENTS

Serves 6

Cheese pastry:
176 g/6 oz plain white flour
75 g/3 oz slightly salted butter
50 g/2 oz Gruyère cheese, grated
1 small egg yolk

For the filling:
2 tbsp olive oil
225 g/8 oz shallots, peeled and halved
1 fennel bulb, trimmed and sliced
1 tsp soft brown sugar
1 medium egg
150 ml/¼ pint double cream
salt and freshly ground black pepper
25 g/1 oz Gruyère cheese, grated
½ tsp ground cinnamon
mixed salad leaves, to serve

TASTY TIP

Fennel has a very aromatic, almost aniseed flavour, which works particularly well with the sweet shallots and the cheese in this dish. A nice addition is to add a generous grating of nutmeg to the pie filling in step 5 as this compliments the creamy cheese filling.

1 Preheat the oven to 200°C/400°F/Gas Mark 6. Sift the flour into a bowl, then rub in the butter, using your fingertips. Stir in the cheese, then add the egg yolk with about 2 tablespoons of cold water. Mix to a firm dough, then knead lightly. Wrap in clingfilm and chill in the refrigerator for 30 minutes.

2 Roll out the pastry on a lightly floured surface and use to line six 10 cm/4 inch individual flan tins or patty tins which are about 2 cm/¾ inch deep.

3 Line the pastry cases with greaseproof paper and fill with baking beans or rice. Bake blind in the preheated oven for about 10 minutes, then remove the paper and beans.

4 Heat the oil in a frying pan, add the shallots and fennel and fry gently for 5 minutes. Sprinkle with the sugar and cook for a further 10 minutes, stirring occasionally until lightly caramelised. Reserve until cooled.

5 Beat together the egg and cream and season to taste with salt and pepper. Divide the shallot mixture between the pastry cases. Pour over the egg mixture and sprinkle with the cheese and cinnamon. Bake for 20 minutes, until golden and set. Serve with the salad leaves.

3

4

5

Red Pepper & Basil Tart

INGREDIENTS

Serves 4-6

For the olive pastry:

225 g/8 oz plain flour
pinch of salt
50 g/2 oz pitted black olives,
  finely chopped
1 medium egg, lightly beaten,
  plus 1 egg yolk
3 tbsp olive oil

For the filling:

2 large red peppers, quartered
  and deseeded
175 g/6 oz mascarpone cheese
4 tbsp milk
2 medium eggs
3 tbsp freshly chopped basil
salt and freshly ground black pepper
sprig of fresh basil, to garnish
mixed salad, to serve

HELPFUL HINT

Pre-baking (or baking blind) the pastry shell before filling ensures that the pastry will not become soggy and that it will be cooked through.

1 Preheat oven to 200°C/400°F/Gas Mark 6, 15 minutes before cooking. Sift the flour and salt into a bowl. Make a well in the centre. Stir together the egg, oil and 1 tablespoon of tepid water. Add to the dry ingredients, drop in the olives and mix to a dough. Knead on a lightly floured surface for a few seconds until smooth, then wrap in clingfilm and chill in the refrigerator for 30 minutes.

2 Roll out the pastry and use to line a 23 cm/9 inch loose-bottomed fluted flan tin. Lightly prick the base with a fork. Cover and chill in the refrigerator for 20 minutes.

3 Cook the peppers under a hot grill for 10 minutes, or until the skins are blackened and blistered. Put the peppers in a plastic bag, cool for 10 minutes, then remove the skin and slice.

4 Line the pastry case with tinfoil or greaseproof paper weighed down with baking beans and bake in the preheated oven for 10 minutes. Remove the tinfoil and beans and bake for a further 5 minutes. Reduce the oven temperature to 180°C/350°F/Gas Mark 4.

5 Beat the mascarpone cheese until smooth. Gradually add the milk and eggs. Stir in the peppers and basil and season to taste with salt and pepper. Spoon into the flan case and bake for 25–30 minutes, or until lightly set. Garnish with a sprig of fresh basil and serve immediately with a mixed salad.

1

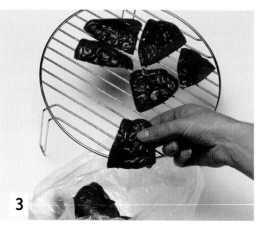

3

5

Roasted Vegetable Pie

INGREDIENTS

Serves 4

225 g/8 oz plain flour
pinch of salt
50 g/2 oz white vegetable fat or lard,
  cut into squares
50 g/2 oz butter, cut into squares
2 tsp herbes de Provence
1 red pepper, deseeded and halved
1 green pepper, deseeded and halved
1 yellow pepper, deseeded and halved
3 tbsp extra virgin olive oil
1 aubergine, trimmed and sliced
1 courgette, trimmed and
  halved lengthways
1 leek, trimmed and cut into chunks
1 medium egg, beaten
125 g/4 oz fresh mozzarella
  cheese, sliced
salt and freshly ground black pepper
sprigs of mixed herbs, to garnish

HELPFUL HINT

When buying mozzarella look out
for the buffalo variety – it has the
best flavour.

1 Preheat the oven to 220°C/425°F/Gas Mark 7. Sift the flour and salt into a large bowl, add the fats and mix lightly. Using your fingertips, rub into the flour until the mixture resembles breadcrumbs. Stir in the herbes de Provence. Sprinkle over a tablespoon of cold water and with a knife start bringing the dough together – it may be necessary to use your hands for the final stage. If the dough does not form a ball instantly, add a little more water. Place the pastry in a polythene bag and chill for 30 minutes.

2 Place the peppers on a baking tray and sprinkle with 1 tablespoon of oil. Roast in the preheated oven for 20 minutes or until the skins start to blacken. Brush the aubergines, courgettes and leeks with oil and place on another baking tray. Roast in the oven with the peppers for 20 minutes.

3 Place the blackened peppers in a polythene bag and leave the skin to loosen for 5 minutes. When cool enough to handle, peel the skins off the peppers.

4 Roll out half the pastry on a lightly floured surface and use to line a 20.5 cm/8 inch round pie dish. Line the pastry with greaseproof paper and fill with baking beans or rice and bake blind for about 10 minutes. Remove the beans and the paper, then brush the base with a little of the beaten egg. Return to the oven for 5 minutes.

5 Layer the cooked vegetables and the cheese in the pastry case, seasoning each layer. Roll out the remaining pastry on a lightly floured surface, and cut out the lid 5 mm/¼ inch wider than the dish. Brush the rim with the beaten egg and lay the pastry lid on top, press to seal. Knock the edges with the back of a knife. Cut a slit in the lid and brush with the beaten egg. Bake for 30 minutes. Transfer to a large serving dish, garnish with sprigs of mixed herbs and serve immediately.

2

3

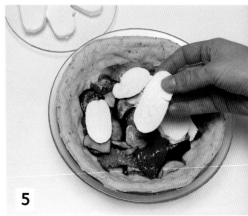

5

Spinach, Pine Nut & Mascarpone Pizza

INGREDIENTS

Serves 2-4

Basic pizza dough:
225 g/8 oz strong plain flour
½ tsp salt
¼ tsp quick-acting dried yeast
150 ml/¼ pint warm water
1 tbsp extra virgin olive oil

For the topping:
3 tbsp olive oil
1 large red onion, peeled and chopped
2 garlic cloves, peeled and finely sliced
450 g/1 lb frozen spinach,
   thawed and drained
salt and freshly ground black pepper
3 tbsp passata
125 g/4 oz mascarpone cheese
1 tbsp toasted pine nuts

FOOD FACT

Traditionally, mozzarella cheese is used for pizza topping, but this recipe incorporates another Italian cheese – mascarpone – which gives a creamy textured result to compliment the delicate spinach and pine nut topping.

1 Preheat the oven to 220°C/425°F/Gas Mark 7. Sift the flour and salt into a bowl and stir in the yeast. Make a well in the centre and gradually add the water and oil to form soft dough.

2 Knead the dough on a floured surface for about 5 minutes until smooth and elastic. Place in a lightly oiled bowl and cover with clingfilm. Leave to rise in a warm place for 1 hour.

3 Knock the pizza dough with your fist a few times, shape and roll out thinly on a lightly floured board. Place on a lightly floured baking sheet and lift the edge to make a little rim. Place another baking sheet into the preheated oven to heat up.

4 Heat half the oil in a frying pan and gently fry the onion and garlic until soft and starting to change colour.

5 Squeeze out any excess water from the spinach and finely chop. Add to the onion and garlic with the remaining olive oil. Season to taste with salt and pepper.

6 Spread the passata on the pizza dough and top with the spinach mixture. Mix the mascarpone with the pine nuts and dot over the pizza.

7 Slide the pizza on to the hot baking sheet and bake for 15–20 minutes. Transfer to a large plate and serve immediately.

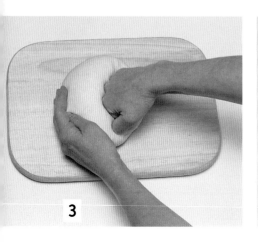

3

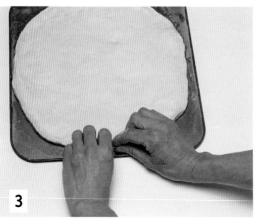

3

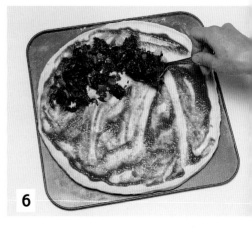

6

Three Tomato Pizza

INGREDIENTS

Serves 2-4

1 quantity pizza dough (see page 28)
3 plum tomatoes
8 cherry tomatoes
6 sun-dried tomatoes
pinch of sea salt
1 tbsp freshly chopped basil
2 tbsp extra virgin olive oil
125 g/4 oz buffalo mozzarella
    cheese, sliced
freshly ground black pepper
fresh basil leaves, to garnish

FOOD FACT

Buffalo mozzarella is considered the king of mozzarellas. It uses buffalo milk, which results in the cheese tasting extremely mild and creamy. A good mozzarella should come in liquid to keep it moist and should tear easily into chunks.

1 Preheat the oven to 220°C/425°F/Gas Mark 7. Place a baking sheet into the oven to heat up.

2 Divide the prepared pizza dough into four equal pieces.

3 Roll out one-quarter of the pizza dough on a lightly floured board to form a 20.5 cm/8 inch round.

4 Lightly cover the three remaining pieces of dough with clingfilm.

5 Roll out the other three pieces into rounds, one at a time. While rolling out any piece of dough, keep the others covered with the clingfilm.

6 Slice the plum tomatoes, halve the cherry tomatoes and chop the sun-dried tomatoes into small pieces.

7 Place a few pieces of each type of tomato on each pizza base then season to taste with the sea salt.

8 Sprinkle with the chopped basil and drizzle with the olive oil. Place a few slices of mozzarella on each pizza and season with black pepper.

9 Transfer the pizza on to the heated baking sheet and cook for 15–20 minutes, or until the cheese is golden brown and bubbling. Garnish with the basil leaves and serve immediately.

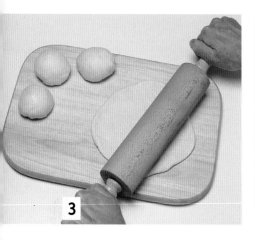
3

7

8

Chargrilled Vegetable & Goats' Cheese Pizza

INGREDIENTS

Serves 4

125 g/4 oz baking potato
1 tbsp olive oil
225 g/8 oz strong white flour
½ tsp salt
1 tsp easy-blend dried yeast

For the topping:

1 medium aubergine, thinly sliced
2 small courgettes, trimmed and
   sliced lengthways
1 yellow pepper, quartered
   and deseeded
1 red onion, peeled and sliced
   into very thin wedges
5 tbsp olive oil
175 g/6 oz cooked new
   potatoes, halved
400 g can chopped tomatoes, drained
2 tsp freshly chopped oregano
125 g/4 oz mozzarella cheese,
   cut into small cubes
125 g/4 oz goats' cheese, crumbled

1 Preheat the oven to 220°C/425°F/Gas Mark 7, 15 minutes before baking. Put a baking sheet in the oven to heat up. Cook the potato in lightly salted boiling water until tender. Peel and mash with the olive oil until smooth.

2 Sift the flour and salt into a bowl. Stir in the yeast. Add the mashed potato and 150 ml/¼ pint warm water and mix to a soft dough. Knead for 5–6 minutes, until smooth. Put the dough in a bowl, cover with clingfilm and leave to rise in a warm place for 30 minutes.

3 To make the topping, arrange the aubergine, courgettes, pepper and onion, skin-side up, on a grill rack and brush with 4 tablespoons of the oil. Grill for 4–5 minutes. Turn the vegetables and brush with the remaining oil. Grill for 3–4 minutes. Cool, skin and slice the pepper. Put all of the vegetables in a bowl, add the halved new potatoes and toss gently together. Set aside.

4 Briefly re-knead the dough then roll out to a 30.5–35.5 cm/12–14 inch round, according to preferred thickness. Mix the tomatoes and oregano together and spread over the pizza base. Scatter over the mozzarella cheese. Put the pizza on the preheated baking sheet and bake for 8 minutes.

5 Arrange the vegetables and goats' cheese on top and bake for 8–10 minutes. Serve immediately.

3

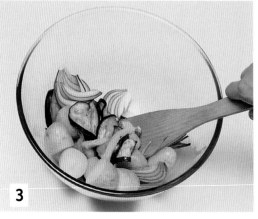

3

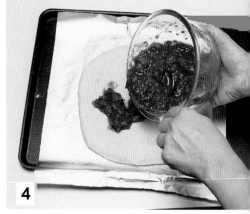

4

Tomato & Courgette Herb Tart

INGREDIENTS

Serves 4

4 tbsp olive oil
1 onion, peeled and finely chopped
3 garlic cloves, peeled and crushed
400 g/14 oz prepared puff pastry,
  thawed if frozen
1 small egg, beaten
2 tbsp freshly chopped rosemary
2 tbsp freshly chopped parsley
175 g/6 oz rindless fresh
  soft goats' cheese
4 ripe plum tomatoes, sliced
1 medium courgette, trimmed
  and sliced
thyme sprigs, to garnish

FOOD FACT

Goats' cheese works particularly well in this recipe, complimenting both the tomato and courgette. Be aware though, that it can tend to be a little acidic, so it is best to try to choose a creamy variety which will mellow even more once baked.

1 Preheat the oven to 230°C/450°F/Gas Mark 8. Heat 2 tablespoons of the oil in a large frying pan.

2 Fry the onion and garlic for about 4 minutes until softened and reserve.

3 Roll out the pastry on a lightly floured surface, and cut out a 30.5 cm/12 inch circle.

4 Brush the pastry with a little beaten egg, then prick all over with a fork.

5 Transfer on to a dampened baking sheet and bake in the preheated oven for 10 minutes.

6 Turn the pastry over and brush with a little more egg. Bake for 5 more minutes, then remove from the oven.

7 Mix together the onion, garlic and herbs with the goats' cheese and spread over the pastry.

8 Arrange the tomatoes and courgettes over the goats' cheese and drizzle with the remaining oil.

9 Bake for 20–25 minutes, or until the pastry is golden brown and the topping is bubbling. Garnish with the thyme sprigs and serve immediately.

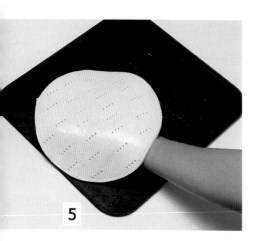
5

7

8

Olive & Feta Parcels

INGREDIENTS

Makes 30

1 small red pepper
1 small yellow pepper
125 g/4 oz assorted marinated
  green and black olives
125 g/4 oz feta cheese
2 tbsp pine nuts, lightly toasted
6 sheets filo pastry
3 tbsp olive oil
sour cream and chive dip, to serve

HELPFUL HINT

Feta is generally made from goats' milk and has quite a salty taste. To make the cheese less salty simply soak it in milk, then drain before eating.

1 Preheat the oven to 180°C/350°F/Gas Mark 4. Preheat the grill, then line the grill rack with tinfoil.

2 Cut the peppers into quarters and remove the seeds. Place skin-side up on the foil-lined grill rack and cook under the preheated grill for 10 minutes, turning occasionally until the skins begin to blacken.

3 Place the peppers in a polythene bag and leave until cool enough to handle, then skin and thinly slice.

4 Chop the olives and cut the feta cheese into small cubes. Mix together the olives, feta, sliced peppers and pine nuts.

5 Cut 1 sheet of filo pastry in half then brush with a little of the oil. Place a spoonful of the olive and feta mix about one-third of the way up the pastry.

6 Fold over the pastry and wrap to form a square parcel encasing the filling completely.

7 Place this parcel in the centre of the second half of the pastry sheet. Brush the edges lightly with a little oil, bring up the corners to meet in the centre and twist them loosely to form a purse.

8 Brush with a little more oil and repeat with the remaining filo pastry and filling.

9 Place the parcels on a lightly oiled baking sheet and bake in the preheated oven for 10–15 minutes, or until crisp and golden brown. Serve with the dip.

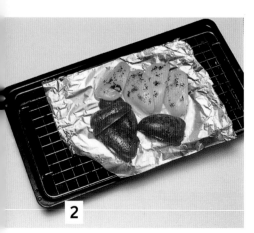

2

5

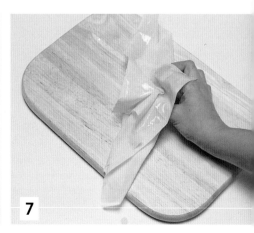

7

Spring Vegetable & Herb Risotto

INGREDIENTS

Serves 2-3

1 litre/1³/₄ pints vegetable stock

125 g/4 oz asparagus tips, trimmed

125 g/4 oz baby carrots, scrubbed

50 g/2 oz peas, fresh or frozen

50 g/2 oz fine French beans, trimmed

1 tbsp olive oil

1 onion, peeled and finely chopped

1 garlic clove, peeled and
finely chopped

2 tsp freshly chopped thyme

225 g/8 oz risotto rice

150 ml/¹/₄ pint white wine

1 tbsp each freshly chopped basil,
chives and parsley

zest of ¹/₂ lemon

3 tbsp crème fraîche

salt and freshly ground black pepper

1 Bring the vegetable stock to the boil in a large saucepan and add the asparagus, baby carrots, peas and beans. Bring the stock back to the boil and remove the vegetables at once using a slotted spoon. Rinse under cold running water. Drain again and reserve. Keep the stock hot.

2 Heat the oil in a large, deep frying pan and add the onion. Cook over a medium heat for 4–5 minutes until starting to brown. Add the garlic and thyme and cook for a further few seconds. Add the rice and stir well for a minute until the rice is hot and coated in oil.

3 Add the white wine and stir constantly until the wine is almost completely absorbed by the rice. Begin adding the stock a ladleful at a time, stirring well and waiting until the last ladleful has been absorbed before stirring in the next. Add the vegetables after using about half of the stock. Continue until all the stock is used. This will take 20–25 minutes. The rice and vegetables should both be tender.

4 Remove the pan from the heat. Stir in the herbs, lemon zest and crème fraîche. Season to taste with salt and pepper and serve immediately.

FOOD FACT

In Italy, they use different types of rice, such as Arborio and Carnaroli, depending on whether the risotto is vegetable, meat or fish-based.

1

3

4

Baby Onion Risotto

INGREDIENTS

Serves 4

For the baby onions:

1 tbsp olive oil

450 g/1 lb baby onions,
  peeled and halved if large

pinch of sugar

1 tbsp freshly chopped thyme

For the risotto:

1 tbsp olive oil

1 small onion, peeled
  and finely chopped

2 garlic cloves, peeled
  and finely chopped

350 g/12 oz risotto rice

150 ml/¼ pint red wine

1 litre/1¾ pints hot vegetable stock

125 g/4 oz soft goats' cheese

salt and freshly ground black pepper

sprigs of fresh thyme, to garnish

rocket leaves, to serve

FOOD FACT

To peel baby onions, put into a saucepan of water and bring to the boil. Drain and run under cold water. The skins will loosen and peel easily.

1 For the baby onions, heat the olive oil in a saucepan and add the onions with the sugar. Cover and cook over a low heat, stirring occasionally, for 20–25 minutes until caramelised. Uncover during the last 10 minutes of cooking.

2 Meanwhile, for the risotto, heat the oil in a large frying pan and add the onion. Cook over a medium heat for 5 minutes until softened. Add the garlic and cook for a further 30 seconds.

3 Add the risotto rice and stir well. Add the red wine and stir constantly until the wine is almost completely absorbed by the rice. Begin adding the stock a ladleful at a time, stirring well and waiting until the last ladleful has been absorbed before stirring in the next. It will take 20–25 minutes to add all the stock by which time the rice should be just cooked but still firm. Remove from the heat.

4 Add the thyme to the onions and cook briefly. Increase the heat and allow the onion mixture to bubble for 2–3 minutes until almost evaporated. Add the onion mixture to the risotto along with the goats' cheese. Stir well and season to taste with salt and pepper. Garnish with sprigs of fresh thyme. Serve immediately with the rocket leaves.

1

3

4

Spiced Couscous & Vegetables

INGREDIENTS

Serves 4

1 tbsp olive oil

1 large shallot, peeled
   and finely chopped

1 garlic clove, peeled
   and finely chopped

1 small red pepper, deseeded and
   cut into strips

1 small yellow pepper,
   deseeded and cut into strips

1 small aubergine, diced

1 tsp each turmeric, ground cumin,
   ground cinnamon and paprika

2 tsp ground coriander

large pinch saffron strands

2 tomatoes, peeled, deseeded
   and diced

2 tbsp lemon juice

225 g/8 oz couscous

225 ml/8 fl oz vegetable stock

2 tbsp raisins

2 tbsp whole almonds

2 tbsp freshly chopped parsley

2 tbsp freshly chopped coriander

salt and freshly ground black pepper

1 Heat the oil in a large frying pan and add the shallot and garlic and cook for 2–3 minutes until softened. Add the peppers and aubergine and reduce the heat.

2 Cook for 8–10 minutes until the vegetables are tender, adding a little water if necessary.

3 Test a piece of aubergine to ensure it is cooked through. Add all the spices and cook for a further minute, stirring.

4 Increase the heat and add the tomatoes and lemon juice. Cook for 2–3 minutes until the tomatoes have started to break down. Remove from the heat and leave to cool slightly.

5 Meanwhile, put the couscous into a large bowl. Bring the stock to the boil in a saucepan, then pour over the couscous. Stir well and cover with a clean tea towel.

6 Leave to stand for 7–8 minutes until all the stock is absorbed and the couscous is tender.

7 Uncover the couscous and fluff with a fork. Stir in the vegetable and spice mixture along with the raisins, almonds, parsley and coriander. Season to taste with salt and pepper and serve.

3

5

7

Black Bean Chilli with Avocado Salsa

INGREDIENTS

Serves 4

250 g/9 oz black beans and black-eye
    beans, soaked overnight
2 tbsp olive oil
1 large onion, peeled
    and finely chopped
1 red pepper, deseeded and diced
2 garlic cloves, peeled
    and finely chopped
1 red chilli, deseeded
    and finely chopped
2 tsp chilli powder
1 tsp ground cumin
2 tsp ground coriander
400 g can chopped tomatoes
450 ml/³/₄ pint vegetable stock
1 small ripe avocado, diced
¹/₂ small red onion, peeled and
    finely chopped
2 tbsp freshly chopped coriander
juice of 1 lime
1 small tomato, peeled, deseeded
    and diced
salt and freshly ground black pepper
25 g/1 oz dark chocolate

To garnish:
crème fraîche
lime slices
sprigs of coriander

1   Drain the beans and place in a large saucepan with at least twice
    their volume of fresh water.

2   Bring slowly to the boil, skimming off any froth that rises to the
    surface. Boil rapidly for 10 minutes, then reduce the heat and
    simmer for about 45 minutes, adding more water if necessary.
    Drain and reserve.

3   Heat the oil in a large saucepan and add the onion and pepper.
    Cook for 3–4 minutes until softened. Add the garlic and chilli. Cook
    for 5 minutes, or until the onion and pepper have softened. Add the
    chilli powder, cumin and coriander and cook for 30 seconds. Add
    the beans along with the tomatoes and stock.

4   Bring to the boil and simmer uncovered for 40–45 minutes until the
    beans and vegetables are tender and the sauce has reduced.

5   Mix together the avocado, onion, fresh coriander, lime juice and
    tomato. Season with salt and pepper and set aside. Remove the
    chilli from the heat. Break the chocolate into pieces. Sprinkle over
    the chilli. Leave for 2 minutes then stir well. Garnish with crème
    fraîche, lime slices and coriander. Serve with the avocado salsa.

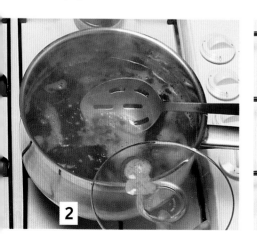

2

3

5

Boston-style Baked Beans

INGREDIENTS

Serves 8

350 g/12 oz mixed dried pulses, e.g. haricot, flageolet, cannellini and pinto beans and chickpeas

1 large onion, peeled and finely chopped

125 g/4 oz black treacle or molasses

2 tbsp Dijon mustard

2 tbsp light brown soft sugar

125 g/4 oz plain flour

150 g/5 oz fine cornmeal

2 tbsp caster sugar

2½ tsp baking powder

½ tsp salt

2 tbsp freshly chopped thyme

2 medium eggs

200 ml/7 fl oz milk

2 tbsp melted butter

salt and freshly ground black pepper

parsley sprigs, to garnish

1 Preheat the oven to 130°C/250°F/Gas Mark ½. Put the pulses into a large saucepan and cover with at least twice their volume of water. Bring to the boil and simmer for 2 minutes. Leave to stand for 1 hour. Return to the boil and boil rapidly for about 10 minutes. Drain and reserve.

2 Mix together the onion, treacle or molasses, mustard and sugar in a large mixing bowl. Add the drained beans and 300 ml/½ pint fresh water. Stir well, bring to the boil, cover and transfer to the preheated oven for 4 hours in an ovenproof dish, stirring once every hour and adding more water if necessary.

3 When the beans are cooked, remove from the oven and keep warm. Increase the oven temperature to 200°C/400°F/Gas Mark 6. Mix together the plain flour, cornmeal, caster sugar, baking powder, salt and most of the thyme, reserving about one third for garnish. In a separate bowl beat the eggs, then stir in the milk and butter. Pour the wet ingredients on to the dry ones and stir just enough to combine.

4 Pour into a buttered 18 cm/7 inch square cake tin. Sprinkle over the remaining thyme. Bake for 30 minutes until golden and risen or until a skewer inserted into the centre comes out clean. Cut into squares, then reheat the beans. Season to taste with salt and pepper and serve immediately, garnished with parsley sprigs.

2

3

4

Pumpkin & Chickpea Curry

INGREDIENTS

Serves 4

1 tbsp vegetable oil

1 small onion, peeled and sliced

2 garlic cloves, peeled
and finely chopped

2.5 cm/1 inch piece root ginger,
peeled and grated

1 tsp ground coriander

½ tsp ground cumin

½ tsp ground turmeric

¼ tsp ground cinnamon

2 tomatoes, chopped

2 red bird's eye chillies, deseeded
and finely chopped

450 g/1 lb pumpkin or butternut
squash flesh, cubed

1 tbsp hot curry paste

300 ml/½ pint vegetable stock

1 large firm banana

400 g can chickpeas, drained
and rinsed

salt and freshly ground black pepper

1 tbsp freshly chopped coriander

coriander sprigs, to garnish

rice or naan bread, to serve

1 Heat 1 tablespoon of the oil in a saucepan and add the onion. Fry gently for 5 minutes until softened.

2 Add the garlic, ginger and spices and fry for a further minute. Add the chopped tomatoes and chillies and cook for another minute.

3 Add the pumpkin and curry paste and fry gently for 3–4 minutes before adding the stock.

4 Stir well, bring to the boil and simmer for 20 minutes until the pumpkin is tender.

5 Thickly slice the banana and add to the pumpkin along with the chickpeas. Simmer for a further 5 minutes.

6 Season to taste with salt and pepper and add the chopped coriander. Serve immediately, garnished with coriander sprigs and some rice or naan bread.

2

3

5

Roasted Mixed Vegetables with Garlic & Herb Sauce

INGREDIENTS

Serves 4

1 large garlic bulb
1 large onion, peeled
  and cut into wedges
4 small carrots, peeled and quartered
4 small parsnips, peeled
6 small potatoes, scrubbed
  and halved
1 fennel bulb, sliced thickly
4 sprigs of fresh rosemary
4 sprigs of fresh thyme
2 tbsp olive oil
salt and freshly ground black pepper
200 g/7 oz low-fat soft cheese with
  herbs and garlic
4 tbsp milk
zest of ½ lemon
sprigs of thyme, to garnish

1   Preheat the oven to 220°C/425°F/Gas Mark 7. Cut the garlic in half horizontally. Put into a large roasting tin with all the vegetables and herbs.

2   Add the oil, season well with salt and pepper and toss together to coat lightly in the oil.

3   Cover with tinfoil and roast in the preheated oven for 50 minutes. Remove the tinfoil and cook for a further 30 minutes until all the vegetables are tender and slightly charred.

4   Remove the tin from the oven and allow to cool.

5   In a small saucepan, melt the low-fat soft cheese together with the milk and lemon zest.

6   Remove the garlic from the roasting tin and squeeze the flesh into a bowl. Mash thoroughly then add to the sauce. Heat through gently. Season the vegetables to taste. Pour some sauce into small ramekins and garnish with 4 sprigs of thyme. Serve immediately with the roasted vegetables and the sauce to dip.

1

3

5

Roasted Butternut Squash

INGREDIENTS

Serves 4

2 small butternut squash
4 garlic cloves, peeled and crushed
1 tbsp olive oil
salt and freshly ground black pepper
1 tbsp walnut oil
4 medium-sized leeks, trimmed,
   cleaned and thinly sliced
1 tbsp black mustard seeds
300 g can cannellini beans,
   drained and rinsed
125 g/4 oz fine French beans, halved
150 ml/¼ pint vegetable stock
50 g/2 oz rocket
2 tbsp freshly snipped chives fresh
   chives, to garnish

To serve:

4 tbsp fromage frais
mixed salad

1 Preheat the oven to 200°C/400°F/Gas Mark 6. Cut the butternut squash in half lengthwise and scoop out all of the seeds.

2 Score the squash in a diamond pattern with a sharp knife. Mix the garlic with the olive oil and brush over the cut surfaces of the squash. Season well with salt and pepper. Put on a baking sheet and roast for 40 minutes until tender.

3 Heat the walnut oil in a saucepan and fry the leeks and mustard seeds for 5 minutes.

4 Add the drained cannellini beans, French beans and vegetable stock. Bring to the boil and simmer gently for 5 minutes until the French beans are tender.

5 Remove from the heat and stir in the rocket and chives. Season well. Remove the squash from the oven and allow to cool for 5 minutes. Spoon in the bean mixture. Garnish with a few snipped chives and serve immediately with the fromage frais and a mixed salad.

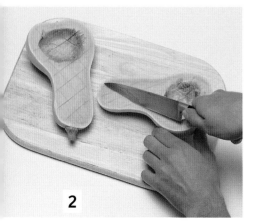

2

3

5

Vegetable Cassoulet

INGREDIENTS

Serves 6

125 g/4 oz dried haricot beans,
   soaked overnight
2 tbsp olive oil
2 garlic cloves, peeled and chopped
225 g/8 oz baby onions,
   peeled and halved
2 carrots, peeled and diced
2 celery sticks, trimmed and
   finely chopped
1 red pepper, deseeded and chopped
175 g/6 oz mixed mushrooms, sliced
1 tbsp each freshly chopped
   rosemary, thyme and sage
150 ml/¼ pint red wine
4 tbsp tomato purée
1 tbsp dark soy sauce
salt and freshly ground black pepper
50 g/2 oz fresh breadcrumbs
1 tbsp freshly chopped parsley
basil sprigs, to garnish

HELPFUL HINT

If cooking dried haricot beans is too time-consuming, then substitute with canned beans instead.

1 Preheat the oven to 190°C/375°F/Gas Mark 5. Drain the haricot beans and place in a saucepan with 1.1 litres/2 pints of fresh water. Bring to the boil and boil rapidly for 10 minutes. Reduce the heat and simmer gently for 45 minutes. Drain the beans, reserving 300 ml/½ pint of the liquid.

2 Heat 1 tablespoon of the oil in a flameproof casserole dish and add the garlic, onions, carrot, celery and red pepper. Cook gently for 10–12 minutes until tender and starting to brown. Add a little water if the vegetables start to stick. Add the mushrooms and cook for a further 5 minutes until softened. Add the herbs and stir briefly.

3 Stir in the red wine and boil rapidly for about 5 minutes until reduced and syrupy. Stir in the reserved beans and their liquid, tomato purée and soy sauce. Season to taste with salt and pepper.

4 Mix together the breadcrumbs and parsley with the remaining 1 tablespoon of oil. Scatter this mixture evenly over the top of the stew. Cover loosely with foil and transfer to the preheated oven. Cook for 30 minutes. Carefully remove the foil and cook for a further 15–20 minutes until the topping is crisp and golden. Serve immediately, garnished with basil sprigs.

2

3

4

Creamy Puy Lentils

INGREDIENTS

Serves 4

225 g/8 oz puy lentils
1 tbsp olive oil
1 garlic clove, peeled and
 finely chopped
zest and juice of 1 lemon
1 tsp whole-grain mustard
1 tbsp freshly chopped tarragon
3 tbsp crème fraîche
salt and freshly ground black pepper
2 small tomatoes, deseeded
 and chopped
50 g/2 oz pitted black olives
1 tbsp freshly chopped parsley

To garnish:

sprigs of fresh tarragon
lemon wedges

FOOD FACT

Puy lentils are smaller and fatter than green lentils and have a pretty mottled colouring, ranging from gold through to green. They keep their shape and firm texture when cooked.

1 Put the lentils in a saucepan with plenty of cold water and bring to the boil.

2 Boil rapidly for 10 minutes, reduce the heat and simmer gently for a further 20 minutes until just tender. Drain well.

3 Meanwhile, prepare the dressing. Heat the oil in a frying pan over a medium heat.

4 Add the garlic and cook for about a minute until just beginning to brown. Add the lemon zest and juice.

5 Add the mustard and cook for a further 30 seconds.

6 Add the tarragon and crème fraîche and season to taste with salt and pepper.

7 Simmer and add the drained lentils, tomatoes and olives.

8 Transfer to a serving dish and sprinkle the chopped parsley on top.

9 Garnish the lentils with the tarragon sprigs and the lemon wedges and serve immediately.

1

4

7

Peperonata

INGREDIENTS

Serves 6

2 red peppers

2 yellow peppers

450 g/1 lb waxy potatoes

1 large onion

2 tbsp good quality virgin olive oil

700 g/1½ lb tomatoes, peeled,
   deseeded and chopped

2 small courgettes

50 g/2 oz pitted black olives, quartered

small handful basil leaves

salt and freshly ground black pepper

crusty bread, to serve

FOOD FACT

This dish is delicious served with Parmesan melba toasts. To make, simply remove the crusts from 4 slices of thin white bread. Lightly toast and allow to cool before splitting each piece in half by slicing horizontally. Cut diagonally into triangles, place under a hot grill and toast each side for a few minutes until golden and curling at the edges. Sprinkle with finely grated fresh Parmesan cheese and melt under the grill.

1 Prepare the peppers by halving them lengthwise and removing the stems, seeds, and membranes.

2 Cut the peppers lengthwise into strips about 1 cm/½ inch wide. Peel the potatoes and cut into rough dice, about 2.5–3 cm/ 1–1¼ inches across. Cut the onion lengthwise into eight wedges.

3 Heat the olive oil in a large saucepan over a medium heat.

4 Add the onion and cook for about 5 minutes, or until starting to brown.

5 Add the peppers, potatoes, tomatoes, courgettes, black olives and about 4 torn basil leaves. Season to taste with salt and pepper.

6 Stir the mixture, cover and cook over a very low heat for about 40 minutes, or until the vegetables are tender but still hold their shape. Garnish with the remaining basil. Transfer to a serving bowl and serve immediately, with chunks of crusty bread.

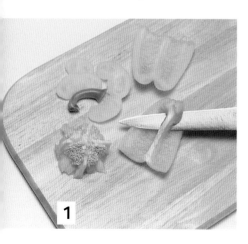

1

4

5

Mushroom Stew

INGREDIENTS

Serves 4

15 g/½ oz dried porcini mushrooms

900 g/2 lb assorted fresh
 mushrooms, wiped

2 tbsp good quality virgin olive oil

1 onion, peeled and finely chopped

2 garlic cloves, peeled and
 finely chopped

1 tbsp fresh thyme leaves

pinch of ground cloves

salt and freshly ground black pepper

700 g/1½ lb tomatoes, peeled,
 deseeded and chopped

225 g/8 oz instant polenta

600ml/1 pint vegetable stock

3 tbsp freshly chopped mixed herbs

sprigs of parsley, to garnish

TASTY TIP

For a dinner party version of this recipe, add a generous splash of vegetarian red wine with the soaking liquid in step 5 and just before serving, remove from the heat and stir in 2 tablespoons of Greek yogurt.

1 Soak the porcini mushrooms in a small bowl of hot water for 20 minutes.

2 Drain, reserving the porcini mushrooms and their soaking liquid. Cut the fresh mushrooms in half and reserve.

3 In a saucepan, heat the oil and add the onion.

4 Cook gently for 5–7 minutes until softened. Add the garlic, thyme and cloves and continue cooking for 2 minutes.

5 Add all the mushrooms and cook for 8–10 minutes until the mushrooms have softened, stirring often. Season to taste with salt and pepper and add the tomatoes and the reserved soaking liquid.

6 Simmer, partly covered, over a low heat for about 20 minutes until thickened. Adjust the seasoning to taste.

7 Meanwhile, cook the polenta according to the packet instructions using the vegetable stock. Stir in the herbs and divide between four dishes.

8 Ladle the mushrooms over the polenta, garnish with the parsley and serve immediately.

5

6

7

Huevos Rancheros

INGREDIENTS

Serves 4

2 tbsp olive oil
1 large onion, peeled
  and finely chopped
1 red pepper, deseeded
  and finely chopped
2 garlic cloves, peeled
  and finely chopped
2–4 green chillies, deseeded and
  finely chopped
1 tsp ground cumin
1 tsp chilli powder
2 tsp ground coriander
2 tbsp freshly chopped coriander
700 g/1½ lb ripe plum
  tomatoes, peeled, deseeded
  and roughly chopped
¼ tsp sugar
8 small eggs
4–8 flour tortillas
salt and freshly ground black pepper
sprigs of fresh coriander, to garnish
refried beans, to serve (optional)

1 Heat the oil in a large heavy-based saucepan. Add the onion and pepper and cook over a medium heat for 10 minutes.

2 Add the garlic, chillies, ground cumin, chilli powder and chopped coriander and cook for a further minute.

3 Add the tomatoes and sugar. Stir well, cover and cook gently for 20 minutes. Uncover and cook for a further 20 minutes.

4 Lightly poach the eggs in a large frying pan, filled with gently simmering water. Drain well and keep warm.

5 Place the tortillas briefly under a preheated hot grill, turning once, then remove from the grill when crisp.

6 Add the freshly chopped coriander to the tomato sauce and season to taste with salt and pepper.

7 To serve, arrange two tortillas on each serving plate, top with two eggs and spoon the sauce over. Garnish with sprigs of fresh coriander and serve immediately with warmed refried beans, if liked.

2

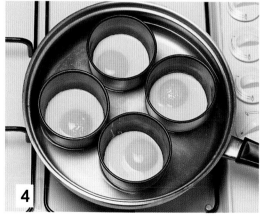

4

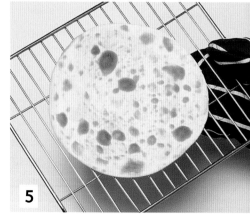

5

Bulghur Wheat Salad with Minty Lemon Dressing

INGREDIENTS

Serves 4

125 g/4 oz bulghur wheat
10 cm /4 inch piece cucumber
2 shallots, peeled
125 g/4 oz baby sweetcorn
3 ripe but firm tomatoes

For the dressing:

grated rind of 1 lemon
3 tbsp lemon juice
3 tbsp freshly chopped mint
2 tbsp freshly chopped parsley
1–2 tsp clear honey
2 tbsp sunflower oil
salt and freshly ground black pepper

FOOD FACT

This dish is loosely based on the Middle Eastern dish tabbouleh, a type of salad in which all the ingredients are mixed together and served cold.

1 Place the bulghur wheat in a saucepan and cover with boiling water.

2 Simmer for about 10 minutes, then drain thoroughly and turn into a serving bowl.

3 Cut the cucumber into small cubes, chop the shallots finely and reserve. Steam the sweetcorn over a pan of boiling water for 10 minutes or until tender. Drain and slice into thick chunks.

4 Cut a cross on the top of each tomato and place in boiling water until their skins start to peel away.

5 Remove the skins and the seeds and cut the tomatoes into small cubes.

6 Make the dressing by briskly whisking all the ingredients in a small bowl until well mixed.

7 When the bulghur wheat has cooled a little, add all the prepared vegetables and stir in the dressing. Season to taste with salt and pepper and serve.

2

3

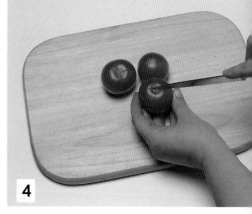

4

Carrot & Parsnip Terrine

INGREDIENTS

Serves 8-10

550 g/1¼ lb carrots, peeled
  and chopped
450 g/1 lb parsnips, peeled
  and chopped
6 tbsp crème fraîche
450 g/1 lb spinach, rinsed
1 tbsp brown sugar
1 tbsp freshly chopped parsley
½ tsp freshly grated nutmeg
salt and freshly ground black pepper
6 medium eggs
sprigs of fresh basil, to garnish

For the tomato coulis:

450 g/1 lb ripe tomatoes,
  deseeded and chopped
1 medium onion, peeled and
  finely chopped

1 Preheat the oven to 200°C/400°F/Gas Mark 6. Oil and line a 900 g/2 lb loaf tin with non-stick baking paper. Cook the carrots and parsnips in boiling salted water for 10–15 minutes or until very tender. Drain and purée separately. Add 2 tablespoons of crème fraîche to both the carrots and the parsnips.

2 Steam the spinach for 5–10 minutes or until very tender. Drain and squeeze out as much liquid as possible, then stir in the remaining crème fraîche.

3 Add the brown sugar to the carrot purée, the parsley to the parsnip mixture and the nutmeg to the spinach. Season all to taste with salt and pepper.

4 Beat 2 eggs, add to the spinach and turn into the prepared tin. Add another 2 beaten eggs to the carrot mixture and layer carefully on top of the spinach. Beat the remaining eggs into the parsnip purée and layer on top of the terrine.

5 Place the tin in a baking dish and pour in enough hot water to come halfway up the sides of the tin. Bake in the preheated oven for 1 hour until a skewer inserted into the centre comes out clean.

6 Leave the terrine to cool for at least 30 minutes. Run a sharp knife around the edges. Turn out on to a dish and reserve.

7 Make the tomato coulis by simmering the tomatoes and onions together for 5–10 minutes until slightly thickened.

8 Season to taste. Blend well in a liquidiser or food processor and serve as an accompaniment to the terrine. Garnish with sprigs of basil and serve.

3

4

7

Warm Fruity Rice Salad

INGREDIENTS

Serves 4

175 g/6 oz mixed basmati and wild rice
300 ml/½ pint vegetable stock
125 g/4 oz ready-to-eat dried apricots
125 g/4 oz ready-to-eat dried dates
3 sticks celery

For the dressing:

2 tbsp sunflower oil
1 tbsp white wine vinegar
4 tbsp lemon juice
1–2 tsp clear honey, warmed
1 tsp Dijon mustard
freshly ground black pepper

To garnish:

6 spring onions
sprigs of fresh coriander

1 Place the rice in a pan of boiling salted water and cook for 15–20 minutes or until tender. Rinse thoroughly with boiling water and reserve.

2 Chop the apricots and dates into small pieces. Peel any tough membranes from the outside of the celery and chop into cubes. Fold the apricots, dates and celery into the warm rice.

3 Make the dressing by whisking all the ingredients together in a small bowl until thoroughly mixed. Pour 2–3 tablespoons over the rice and stir in gently and evenly. Serve the remaining dressing separately.

4 Trim and chop the spring onions. Sprinkle the spring onions over the top of the salad and garnish with the sprigs of coriander. Serve while still warm.

2

6

Hot & Spicy Red Cabbage with Apples

INGREDIENTS

Serves 8

900 g/2 lb red cabbage,
   cored and shredded
450 g/1 lb onions, peeled
   and finely sliced
450 g/1 lb cooking apples, peeled,
   cored and finely sliced
½ tsp mixed spice
1 tsp ground cinnamon
2 tbsp soft light brown sugar
salt and freshly ground black pepper
grated rind of 1 large orange
1 tbsp fresh orange juice
50 ml/2 fl oz medium sweet cider
   (or apple juice)
2 tbsp wine vinegar

To serve:

crème fraîche
freshly ground black pepper

TASTY TIP

Try balsamic vinegar instead of wine vinegar in this recipe – it has a soft, sweet and sour, slightly fuller taste that works particularly well with the spices in this recipe.

1 Preheat the oven to 150°C/300°F/Gas Mark 2. Put just enough cabbage in a large casserole dish to cover the base evenly.

2 Place a layer of the onions and apples on top of the cabbage.

3 Sprinkle a little of the mixed spice, cinnamon and sugar over the top. Season with salt and pepper.

4 Spoon over a small portion of the orange rind, orange juice and the cider.

5 Continue to layer the casserole dish with the ingredients in the same order until used up.

6 Pour the vinegar as evenly as possible over the top layer of the ingredients.

7 Cover the casserole dish with a close-fitting lid and bake in the preheated oven for 2 hours, stirring occasionally, until the cabbage is moist and tender. Serve immediately with the crème fraîche and black pepper.

2

3

7

Marinated Vegetable Kebabs

INGREDIENTS

Serves 4

2 small courgettes, cut into
   2 cm/³/₄ inch pieces
¹/₂ green pepper, deseeded and cut
   into 2.5 cm/1 inch pieces
¹/₂ red pepper, deseeded and cut into
   2.5 cm/1 inch pieces
¹/₂ yellow pepper, deseeded and cut
   into 2.5 cm/1 inch pieces
8 baby onions, peeled
8 button mushrooms
8 cherry tomatoes
freshly chopped parsley, to garnish
freshly cooked couscous, to serve

For the marinade:

1 tbsp light olive oil
4 tbsp dry sherry
2 tbsp light soy sauce
1 red chilli, deseeded and
   finely chopped
2 garlic cloves, peeled and crushed
2.5 cm/1 inch piece root ginger,
   peeled and finely grated

1 Place the courgettes, peppers and baby onions in a pan of just-boiled water. Bring back to the boil and simmer for about 30 seconds.

2 Drain and rinse the cooked vegetables in cold water and dry on absorbent kitchen paper.

3 Thread the cooked vegetables and the mushrooms and tomatoes alternately on to skewers and place in a large shallow dish.

4 Make the marinade by whisking all the ingredients together until thoroughly blended. Pour the marinade evenly over the kebabs, then chill in the refrigerator for at least 1 hour. Spoon the marinade over the kebabs occasionally during this time.

5 Place the kebabs in a hot griddle pan or on a hot barbecue and cook gently for 10–12 minutes. Turn the kebabs frequently and brush with the marinade when needed. When the vegetables are tender, sprinkle over the chopped parsley and serve immediately with couscous.

3

4

5

Pumpkin Pâté

INGREDIENTS

Serves 8-10

450 g/1 lb fresh pumpkin flesh
  (when in season), peeled, or 425 g
  can pumpkin purée
1 tsp sunflower oil
1 small onion, peeled and
  finely chopped
½ orange pepper, deseeded
  and finely chopped
2 medium eggs, beaten
3 tbsp natural yogurt
125 g/4 oz hard cheese
  (such as Edam or Gouda), grated
50 g/2 oz wheatgerm
1 tbsp freshly chopped oregano
salt and freshly ground black pepper
fresh salad leaves and crusty bread,
  to serve

TASTY TIP

This pâté, after being mixed together in step 4, could also be used to stuff fresh pasta. Serve the pasta tossed in a little extra virgin olive oil and some roughly torn fresh sage leaves.

1 Preheat the oven to 180°C/350°F/Gas Mark 4. Oil and line a 900 ml/1½ pint oblong dish or loaf tin. Cut the pumpkin flesh into cubes and place in a pan of boiling water.

2 Simmer for 20 minutes or until the pumpkin is very tender. Drain and leave to cool, then mash well to form a purée.

3 Heat the oil in a non-stick frying pan and cook the chopped onion and pepper for about 4 minutes, until softened.

4 Mix together the puréed pumpkin, softened vegetables, eggs and yogurt. Add the cheese, wheatgerm and chopped oregano. Season well with salt and pepper.

5 When the pumpkin mixture is well blended, spoon it into the prepared tin and stand in a baking dish. Fill the tray with hot water to come halfway up the sides of the tin and carefully place in the preheated oven.

6 Bake for about 1 hour or until firm, then leave to cool. Chill for 30 minutes before turning out on to a serving plate. Serve with crusty bread and a fresh salad.

2

3

4

Spanish Baked Tomatoes

INGREDIENTS

Serves 4

175 g/6 oz whole-grain rice
600 ml/1 pint vegetable stock
2 tsp sunflower oil
2 shallots, peeled and finely chopped
1 garlic clove, peeled and crushed
1 green pepper, deseeded and cut
    into small dice
1 red chilli, deseeded and
    finely chopped
50 g/2 oz button mushrooms
    finely chopped
1 tbsp freshly chopped oregano
salt and freshly ground black pepper
4 large ripe beef tomatoes
1 large egg, beaten
1 tsp caster sugar
basil leaves, to garnish
crusty bread, to serve

1 Preheat the oven to 180°C/350°F/Gas Mark 4. Place the rice in a saucepan, pour over the vegetable stock and bring to the boil. Simmer for 30 minutes or until the rice is tender. Drain and turn into a mixing bowl.

2 Add 1 teaspoon of sunflower oil to a small non-stick pan and gently fry the shallots, garlic, pepper, chilli and mushrooms for 2 minutes. Add to the rice with the chopped oregano. Season with plenty of salt and pepper.

3 Slice the top off each tomato. Cut and scoop out the flesh, removing the hard core. Pass the tomato flesh through a sieve. Add 1 tablespoon of the juice to the rice mixture. Stir in the beaten egg and mix. Sprinkle a little sugar in the base of each tomato. Pile the rice mixture into the shells.

4 Place the tomatoes in a baking dish and pour a little cold water around them. Replace their lids and drizzle a few drops of sunflower oil over the tops.

5 Bake in the preheated oven for about 25 minutes. Garnish with the basil leaves and season with black pepper and serve immediately with crusty bread.

2

3

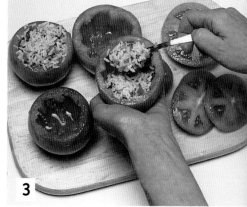
3

Stuffed Onions with Pine Nuts

INGREDIENTS

Serves 4

4 medium onions, peeled

2 garlic cloves, peeled and crushed

2 tbsp fresh brown breadcrumbs

2 tbsp white breadcrumbs

25 g/1 oz sultanas

25 g/1 oz pine nuts

50 g/2 oz hard cheese
  such as Edam, grated

2 tbsp freshly chopped parsley

1 medium egg, beaten

salt and freshly ground black pepper

salad leaves, to serve

1 Preheat the oven to 200°C/400°F/Gas Mark 6. Bring a pan of water to the boil, add the onions and cook gently for about 15 minutes.

2 Drain well. Allow the onions to cool, then slice each one in half horizontally.

3 Scoop out most of the onion flesh but leave a reasonably firm shell.

4 Chop up 4 tablespoons of the onion flesh and place in a bowl with the crushed garlic, breadcrumbs, sultanas, pine nuts, grated cheese and parsley.

5 Mix the breadcrumb mixture together thoroughly. Bind together with as much of the beaten egg as necessary to make a firm filling. Season to taste with salt and pepper.

6 Pile the mixture back into the onion shells and top with the grated cheese. Place on a oiled baking tray and cook in the preheated oven for 20–30 minutes or until golden brown. Serve immediately with the salad leaves.

FOOD FACT

While this dish is delicious on its own, it also compliments barbecued vegetables. The onion takes on a mellow, nutty flavour when baked.

3

4

6

Warm Leek & Tomato Salad

INGREDIENTS

Serves 4

450 g/1 lb trimmed baby leeks
225 g/8 oz ripe, but firm tomatoes
2 shallots, peeled and cut
  into thin wedges

For the honey and lime dressing:

2 tbsp clear honey
grated rind of 1 lime
4 tbsp lime juice
1 tbsp light olive oil
1 tsp Dijon mustard
salt and freshly ground black pepper

To garnish:

freshly chopped tarragon
freshly chopped basil

1 Trim the leeks so that they are all the same length. Place in a steamer over a pan of boiling water and steam for 8 minutes or until just tender.

2 Drain the leeks thoroughly and arrange in a shallow serving dish.

3 Make a cross in the top of the tomatoes, place in a bowl and cover them with boiling water until their skins start to peel away. Remove from the bowl and carefully remove the skins.

4 Cut the tomatoes into four and remove the seeds, then chop into small dice. Spoon over the top of the leeks together with the shallots.

5 In a small bowl make the dressing by whisking the honey, lime rind, lime juice, olive oil, mustard and salt and pepper. Pour 3 tablespoons of the dressing over the leeks and tomatoes and garnish with the tarragon and basil. Serve while the leeks are still warm, with the remaining dressing served separately.

HELPFUL HINT

An easy way to measure out honey is to plunge a metal measuring spoon into boiling water. Drain the spoon, then dip into the honey.

1

3

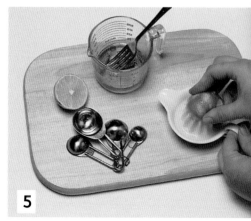
5

Mediterranean Feast

INGREDIENTS

Serves 4

1 small iceberg lettuce
225 g/8 oz French beans
225 g/8 oz baby new
  potatoes, scrubbed
4 medium eggs
1 green pepper
1 medium onion, peeled
50 g/2 oz hard cheese, such as Edam,
  cut into small cubes
8 ripe but firm cherry
  tomatoes, quartered
50 g/2 oz black pitted olives, halved
freshly chopped basil, to garnish

For the lime vinaigrette:

3 tbsp light olive oil
2 tbsp white wine vinegar
4 tbsp lime juice
grated rind of 1 lime
1 tsp Dijon mustard
1-2 tsp caster sugar
salt and freshly ground black pepper

1. Cut the lettuce into four and remove the hard core. Tear into bite-sized pieces and arrange on a large serving platter or 4 individual plates.

2. Cook the French beans in boiling salted water for 8 minutes and the potatoes for 10 minutes or until tender. Drain and rinse in cold water until cool, then cut both the beans and potatoes in half with a sharp knife.

3. Boil the eggs for 10 minutes, then rinse thoroughly under a cold running tap until cool. Remove the shells under water and cut each egg into four.

4. Remove the seeds from the pepper and cut into thin strips and finely chop the onion.

5. Arrange the beans, potatoes, eggs, peppers and onion on top of the lettuce. Add the cheese and tomatoes. Sprinkle over the olives and garnish with the basil.

6. To make the vinaigrette, place all the ingredients in a screw-topped jar and shake vigorously until everything is mixed thoroughly. Spoon 4 tablespoons over the top of the prepared salad and serve the remainder separately.

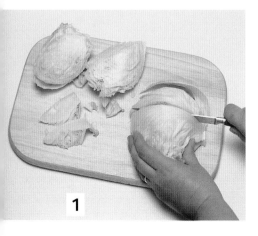

1

4

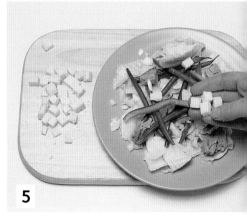

5

Beetroot & Potato Medley

INGREDIENTS

Serves 4

350 g/12 oz raw baby beetroot
½ tsp sunflower oil
225 g/8 oz new potatoes
½ cucumber, peeled
3 tbsp white wine vinegar
150 ml/5 fl oz natural yogurt
salt and freshly ground black pepper
fresh salad leaves
1 tbsp freshly snipped chives,
  to garnish

1 Preheat the oven to 180°C/350°F/Gas Mark 4. Scrub the beetroot thoroughly and place on a baking tray.

2 Brush the beetroot with a little oil and cook for 1½ hours or until a skewer is easily insertable into the beetroot. Allow to cool a little, then remove the skins.

3 Cook the potatoes in boiling water for about 10 minutes. Rinse in cold water and drain. Reserve the potatoes until cool. Dice evenly.

4 Cut the cucumber into cubes and place in a mixing bowl. Chop the beetroot into small cubes and add to the bowl with the reserved potatoes. Gently mix the vegetables together.

5 Mix together the vinegar and yogurt and season to taste with a little salt and pepper. Pour over the vegetables and combine gently.

6 Arrange on a bed of salad leaves garnished with the snipped chives and serve.

HELPFUL HINT

Beetroot can also be cooked in the microwave. Place in a microwaveable bowl. Add sufficient water to come halfway up the sides of the bowl. Cover and cook for 10–15 minutes on high, then leave for 5 minutes before removing the paper. Cook before peeling.

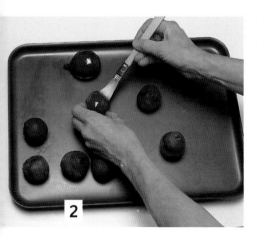
2

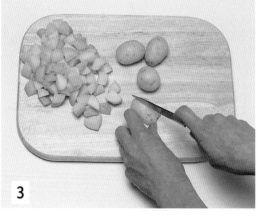
3

4

Light Ratatouille

INGREDIENTS

Serves 4

1 red pepper
2 courgettes, trimmed
1 small aubergine, trimmed
1 onion, peeled
2 ripe tomatoes
50 g/2 oz button mushrooms, wiped
   and halved or quartered
200 ml/7 fl oz tomato juice
1 tbsp freshly chopped basil
salt and freshly ground
   black pepper

1 Deseed the peppers, remove the membrane with a small sharp knife and cut into small cubes. Thickly slice the courgettes and cut the aubergine into small cubes. Slice the onion into rings.

2 Place the tomatoes in boiling water until their skins begin to peel away.

3 Remove the skins from the tomatoes, cut into quarters and remove the seeds.

4 Place all the vegetables in a saucepan with the tomato juice and basil. Season to taste with salt and pepper.

5 Bring to the boil, cover and simmer for 15 minutes or until the vegetables are tender.

6 Remove the vegetables with a slotted spoon and arrange in a serving dish.

7 Bring the liquid in the pan to the boil and boil for 20 seconds until it is slightly thickened. Season the sauce to taste with salt and pepper.

8 Pass the sauce through a sieve to remove some of the seeds and pour over the vegetables. Serve the ratatouille hot or cold.

TASTY TIP

This dish is delicious in an omelette or as a jacket potato filling.

1

4

6

Sicilian Baked Aubergine

INGREDIENTS

Serves 4

1 large aubergine, trimmed

2 celery stalks, trimmed

4 large ripe tomatoes

1 tsp sunflower oil

2 shallots, peeled and finely chopped

1½ tsp tomato purée

25 g/1 oz green pitted olives

25 g/1 oz black pitted olives

salt and freshly ground black pepper

1 tbsp white wine vinegar

2 tsp caster sugar

1 tbsp freshly chopped basil, to garnish

mixed salad leaves, to serve

FOOD FACT

It has been suggested that foods that are purple in colour, such as aubergines, have particularly powerful antioxidants, which help the body to protect itself from disease.

1 Preheat the oven to 200°C/400°F/Gas Mark 6. Cut the aubergine into small cubes and place on an oiled baking tray.

2 Cover the tray with tinfoil and bake in the preheated oven for 15–20 minutes until soft. Reserve, to allow the aubergine to cool.

3 Place the celery and tomatoes in a large bowl and cover with boiling water.

4 Remove the tomatoes from the bowl when their skins begin to peel away. Remove the skins, then deseed and chop the flesh into small pieces.

5 Remove the celery from the bowl of water, finely chop and reserve.

6 Pour the vegetable oil into a non-stick saucepan, add the chopped shallots and fry gently for 2–3 minutes until soft. Add the celery, tomatoes, tomato purée and olives. Season to taste with salt and pepper.

7 Simmer gently for 3–4 minutes. Add the vinegar, sugar and cooled aubergine to the pan and heat gently for 2–3 minutes until all the ingredients are well blended. Reserve to allow the aubergine mixture to cool. When cool, garnish with the chopped basil and serve cold with salad leaves.

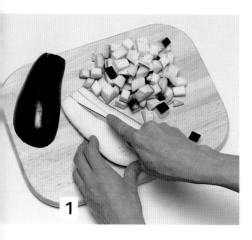

1

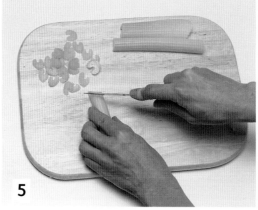

5

6

Leek & Potato Tart

INGREDIENTS

Serves 6

225 g/8 oz plain flour
pinch of salt
150 g/5 oz butter, cubed
50 g/2 oz walnuts, very finely chopped
1 large egg yolk

For the filling:

450 g/1 lb leeks, trimmed
    and thinly sliced
40 g/1½ oz butter
450 g/1 lb large new
    potatoes, scrubbed
300 ml/½ pint soured cream
3 medium eggs, lightly beaten
175 g/6 oz Gruyère cheese, grated
freshly grated nutmeg
salt and freshly ground black pepper
fresh chives, to garnish

TASTY TIP

As an alternative, flavour the pastry with different nuts, such as hazelnuts or almonds, or replace the nuts with 3 tablespoons of freshly chopped mixed herbs.

1. Preheat the oven to 200°C/400°F/Gas Mark 6, about 15 minutes before baking. Sift the flour and salt into a bowl. Rub in the butter until the mixture resembles breadcrumbs. Stir in the nuts. Mix together the egg yolk and 3 tablespoons of cold water. Sprinkle over the dry ingredients and mix to form a dough.

2. Knead on a lightly floured surface for a few seconds, then wrap in clingfilm and chill in the refrigerator for 20 minutes. Roll out and use to line a 20.5 cm/8 inch spring-form tin or very deep flan tin. Chill for a further 30 minutes.

3. Cook the leeks in the butter over a high heat for 2–3 minutes, stirring constantly. Lower the heat, cover and cook for 25 minutes until soft, stirring occasionally. Remove the leeks from the heat.

4. Cook the potatoes in boiling salted water for 15 minutes, or until almost tender. Drain and thickly slice. Add to the leeks. Stir the soured cream into the leeks and potatoes, followed by the eggs, cheese, nutmeg and salt and pepper. Pour into the pastry case and bake on the middle shelf in the preheated oven for 20 minutes.

5. Reduce the oven temperature to 190°C/375°F/Gas Mark 5 and cook for a further 30–35 minutes, or until the filling is set. Garnish with chives and serve immediately.

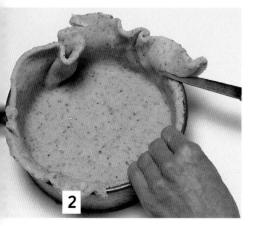

2

3

4

Vegetarian Cassoulet

INGREDIENTS

Serves 4

225 g/8 oz dried haricot beans,
   soaked overnight
2 medium onions
1 bay leaf
1.4 litres/2½ pints cold water
550 g/1¼ lb large potatoes, peeled
   and cut into 1 cm/½ inch slices
salt and freshly ground black pepper
5 tsp olive oil
1 large garlic clove, peeled
   and crushed
2 leeks, trimmed and sliced
200 g can chopped tomatoes
1 tsp dark muscovado sugar
1 tbsp freshly chopped thyme
2 tbsp freshly chopped parsley
3 courgettes, trimmed and sliced

For the topping:
50 g/2 oz fresh white breadcrumbs
25 g/1oz Cheddar cheese, finely grated

1. Preheat the oven to 180°C/350°F/Gas Mark 4, 10 minutes before required. Drain the beans, rinse under cold running water and put in a saucepan. Peel 1 of the onions and add to the beans with the bay leaf. Pour in the water.

2. Bring to a rapid boil and cook for 10 minutes, then turn down the heat, cover and simmer for 50 minutes, or until the beans are almost tender. Drain the beans, reserving the liquor, but discarding the onion and bay leaf.

3. Cook the potatoes in a saucepan of lightly salted boiling water for 6–7 minutes, until almost tender when tested with the point of a knife. Drain and reserve.

4. Peel and chop the remaining onion. Heat the oil in a frying pan and cook the onion with the garlic and leeks for 10 minutes until softened. Stir in the tomatoes, sugar, thyme and parsley. Stir in the beans, with 300 ml/½ pint of the reserved liquor and season to taste. Simmer, uncovered, for 5 minutes.

5. Layer the potato slices, courgettes and ladlefuls of the bean mixture in a large flameproof casserole dish. To make the topping, mix together the breadcrumbs and cheese and sprinkle over the top.

6. Bake in the preheated oven for 40 minutes, or until the vegetables are cooked through and the topping is golden brown and crisp. Serve immediately.

1

4

5

Sweet Potato Cakes with Mango & Tomato Salsa

INGREDIENTS

Serves 4

700 g/1½ lb sweet potatoes, peeled and cut into large chunks
salt and freshly ground black pepper
25 g/1 oz butter
1 onion, peeled and chopped
1 garlic clove, peeled and crushed
pinch of freshly grated nutmeg
1 medium egg, beaten
50 g/2 oz quick-cook polenta
2 tbsp sunflower oil

For the salsa:

1 ripe mango, peeled, stoned and diced
6 cherry tomatoes, cut in wedges
4 spring onions, trimmed and thinly sliced
1 red chilli, deseeded and finely chopped
finely grated rind and juice of ½ lime
2 tbsp freshly chopped mint
1 tsp clear honey
salad leaves, to serve

1 Steam or cook the sweet potatoes in lightly salted boiling water for 15–20 minutes, until tender. Drain well, then mash until smooth.

2 Melt the butter in a saucepan. Add the onion and garlic and cook gently for 10 minutes until soft. Add to the mashed sweet potato and season with the nutmeg, salt and pepper. Stir together until mixed thoroughly. Leave to cool.

3 Shape the mixture into four oval potato cakes, about 2.5 cm/1 inch thick. Dip first in the beaten egg, allowing the excess to fall back into the bowl, then coat in the polenta. Refrigerate for at least 30 minutes.

4 Meanwhile, mix together all the ingredients for the salsa. Spoon into a serving bowl, cover with clingfilm and leave at room temperature to allow the flavours to develop.

5 Heat the oil in a frying pan and cook the potato cakes for 4–5 minutes on each side. Serve with the salsa and salad leaves.

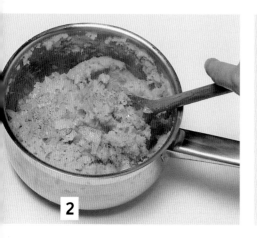

2

3

4

Cheese & Onion Oat Pie

INGREDIENTS

Serves 4

1 tbsp sunflower oil, plus 1 tsp
25 g/1 oz butter
2 medium onions, peeled and sliced
1 garlic clove, peeled and crushed
150 g/5 oz porridge oats
125 g/4 oz mature Cheddar
  cheese, grated
2 medium eggs, lightly beaten
2 tbsp freshly chopped parsley
salt and freshly ground black pepper
275 g/10 oz baking potato, peeled

TASTY TIP

To add flavour to this dish, cook the onions very slowly until soft and just beginning to colour and caramelise – either white or red onions can be used. For a crunchier texture, add 50 g/2 oz chopped hazelnuts instead of 50 g/2 oz of the oats, adding them to the baking sheet of oats for the last 5 minutes of cooking time, in step 2.

1. Preheat the oven to 180°C/350°F/Gas Mark 4. Heat the oil and half the butter in a saucepan until melted. Add the onions and garlic and gently cook for 10 minutes, or until soft. Remove from the heat and tip into a large bowl.

2. Spread the oats out on a baking sheet and toast in the hot oven for 12 minutes. Leave to cool, then add to the onions with the cheese, eggs and parsley. Season to taste with salt and pepper and mix well.

3. Line the base of a 20.5 cm/8 inch round sandwich tin with greaseproof paper and oil well. Thinly slice the potato and arrange the slices on the base, overlapping them slightly.

4. Spoon the cheese and oat mixture on top of the potato, spreading evenly with the back of a spoon. Cover with tinfoil and bake for 30 minutes.

5. Invert the pie onto a baking sheet so that the potatoes are on top. Carefully remove the tin and lining paper.

6. Preheat the grill to medium. Melt the remaining butter and carefully brush over the potato topping. Cook under the preheated grill for 5–6 minutes until the potatoes are lightly browned. Cut into wedges and serve.

2

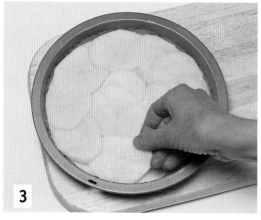

3

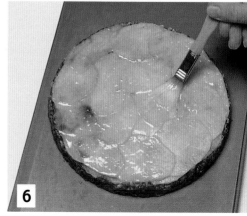

6

Chunky Vegetable & Fennel Goulash with Dumplings

INGREDIENTS

Serves 4

2 fennel bulbs, weighing
   about 450 g/1 lb
2 tbsp sunflower oil
1 large onion, peeled and sliced
1½ tbsp paprika
1 tbsp plain flour
300 ml/½ pint vegetable stock
400 g can chopped tomatoes
450 g/1 lb potatoes, peeled and cut
   into 2.5 cm/1 inch chunks
125 g/4 oz small button mushrooms
salt and freshly ground black pepper

For the dumplings:

1 tbsp sunflower oil
1 small onion, peeled and
   finely chopped
1 medium egg
3 tbsp milk
3 tbsp freshly chopped parsley
125 g/4 oz fresh white breadcrumbs

TASTY TIP

Soured cream or crème fraîche would be delicious if spooned on top of the goulash.

1   Cut the fennel bulbs in half widthways. Thickly slice the stalks and cut the bulbs into eight wedges. Heat the oil in a large saucepan or flameproof casserole dish. Add the onion and fennel and cook gently for 10 minutes until soft. Stir in the paprika and flour.

2   Remove from the heat and gradually stir in the stock. Add the chopped tomatoes, potatoes and mushrooms. Season to taste with salt and pepper. Bring to the boil, reduce the heat and simmer for 20 minutes.

3   Meanwhile, make the dumplings. Heat the oil in a frying pan and gently cook the onion for 10 minutes, until soft. Leave to cool for a few minutes.

4   In a bowl, beat the egg and milk together, then add the onion, parsley, breadcrumbs, and season to taste. With damp hands form the breadcrumb mixture into 12 round dumplings, each about the size of a walnut.

5   Arrange the dumplings on top of the goulash. Cover and cook for a further 15 minutes, until the dumplings are cooked and the vegetables are tender. Serve immediately.

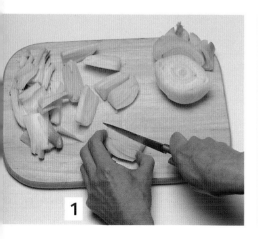

1

2

4

Cabbage Timbale

INGREDIENTS

Serves 4-6

1 small savoy cabbage, weighing
about 350 g/12 oz
salt and freshly ground black pepper
2 tbsp olive oil
1 leek, trimmed and chopped
1 garlic clove, peeled and crushed
75 g/3 oz long-grain rice
200 g can chopped tomatoes
300 ml/½ pint vegetable stock
400 g can flageolet beans,
drained and rinsed
75 g/3 oz Cheddar cheese, grated
1 tbsp freshly chopped oregano

To garnish:

Greek yogurt with paprika
tomato wedges

HANDY HINT

Avoid red or white cabbage for this recipe as their leaves are not flexible enough.

1 Preheat the oven to 180°C/350°F/Gas Mark 4, 10 minutes before required. Remove six of the outer leaves of the cabbage. Cut off the thickest part of the stalk and blanch the leaves in lightly salted boiling water for 2 minutes. Lift out with a slotted spoon and briefly rinse under cold water and reserve.

2 Remove the stalks from the rest of the cabbage leaves. Shred the leaves and blanch in the boiling water for 1 minute. Drain, rinse under cold water and pat dry on absorbent kitchen paper.

3 Heat the oil in a frying pan and cook the leek and garlic for 5 minutes. Stir in the rice, chopped tomatoes with their juice and stock. Bring to the boil, cover and simmer for 15 minutes.

4 Remove the lid and simmer for a further 4–5 minutes, stirring frequently, until the liquid is absorbed and the rice is tender. Stir in the flageolet beans, cheese and oregano. Season to taste with salt and pepper.

5 Line an oiled 1.1 litre/2 pint pudding basin with some of the large cabbage leaves, over-lapping them slightly. Fill the basin with alternate layers of rice mixture and shredded leaves, pressing down well.

6 Cover the top with the remaining leaves. Cover with oiled tinfoil and bake in the preheated for 30 minutes. Leave to stand for 10 minutes. Turn out, cut into wedges and serve with yogurt sprinkled with paprika and tomato wedges.

1

4

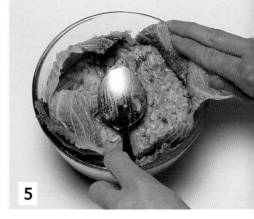
5

Layered Cheese & Herb Potato Cake

INGREDIENTS

Serves 4

900 g/2 lb waxy potatoes
3 tbsp freshly snipped chives
2 tbsp freshly chopped parsley
225 g/8 oz mature Cheddar cheese
2 large egg yolks
1 tsp paprika
125 g/4 oz fresh white breadcrumbs
50 g/2 oz almonds, toasted and
  roughly chopped
50 g/2 oz butter, melted
salt and freshly ground black pepper
mixed salad or steamed vegetables,
  to serve

HANDY HINT

Check that the potatoes are tender all the way through by pushing a thin skewer through the centre. If the potatoes are still a little hard and the top is already brown enough, loosely cover with a piece of tinfoil and continue cooking until done.

1 Preheat the oven to 180°C/350°F/Gas Mark 4. Lightly oil and line the base of a 20.5 cm/8 inch round cake tin with lightly oiled greaseproof or baking parchment paper. Peel and thinly slice the potatoes and reserve. Stir the chives, parsley, cheese and egg yolks together in a small bowl and reserve. Mix the paprika into the breadcrumbs.

2 Sprinkle the almonds over the base of the lined tin. Cover with half the potatoes, arranging them in layers, then sprinkle with the paprika breadcrumb mixture and season to taste with salt and pepper.

3 Spoon the cheese and herb mixture over the breadcrumbs with a little more seasoning, then arrange the remaining potatoes on top. Drizzle over the melted butter and press the surface down firmly.

4 Bake in the preheated oven for 1¼ hours, or until golden and cooked through. Let the tin stand for 10 minutes before carefully turning out and serving in thick wedges. Serve immediately with salad or freshly cooked vegetables.

1

2

3

Rice Nuggets in Herby Tomato Sauce

INGREDIENTS

Serves 4

600 ml/1 pint vegetable stock
1 bay leaf
175 g/6 oz Arborio rice
50 g/2 oz Cheddar cheese, grated
1 medium egg yolk
1 tbsp plain flour
2 tbsp freshly chopped parsley
salt and freshly ground black pepper
grated Parmesan cheese, to serve

For the herby tomato sauce:

1 tbsp olive oil
1 onion, peeled and thinly sliced
1 garlic clove, peeled and crushed
1 small yellow pepper, deseeded
  and diced
400 g can chopped tomatoes
1 tbsp freshly chopped basil

HELPFUL HINT

It is important that the stock is absorbed completely by the rice if these nuggets are to hold their shape. Stir all the time for the last minute of cooking to prevent the rice from sticking or burning.

1 Pour the stock into a large saucepan and add the bay leaf. Bring to the boil, add the rice, stir, then cover and simmer for 15 minutes.

2 Uncover, reduce the heat to low and cook for a further 5 minutes until the rice is tender and all the stock is absorbed, stirring frequently towards the end of cooking time. Allow to cool.

3 Stir the cheese, egg yolk, flour and parsley into the rice. Season to taste, then shape into 20 walnut-sized balls. Cover and refrigerate.

4 To make the sauce, heat the oil in a large frying pan and cook the onion for 5 minutes. Add the garlic and yellow pepper and cook for a further 5 minutes, until soft.

5 Stir in the chopped tomatoes and simmer gently for 3 minutes. Stir in the chopped basil and season to taste.

6 Add the rice nuggets to the sauce and simmer for a further 10 minutes, or until the rice nuggets are cooked through and the sauce has reduced a little. Spoon onto serving plates and serve hot, sprinkled with grated Parmesan cheese.

1

3

6

Mixed Grain Pilaf

INGREDIENTS

Serves 4

2 tbsp olive oil

1 garlic clove, peeled and crushed

½ tsp ground turmeric

125 g/4 oz mixed long-grain
   and wild rice

50 g/2 oz red lentils

300 ml/½ pint vegetable stock

200 g can chopped tomatoes

5 cm/2 inch piece cinnamon stick

salt and freshly ground black pepper

400 g can mixed beans, drained
   and rinsed

15 g/½ oz butter

1 bunch spring onions, trimmed and
   finely sliced

3 medium eggs

4 tbsp freshly chopped herbs, such
   as parsley and chervil

sprigs of fresh dill, to garnish

HELPFUL HINT

Long-grain rice and wild rice have different cooking times, but in ready-mixed packets the rice has been treated to even out the cooking times, making preparation simpler.

1   Heat 1 tablespoon of the oil in a saucepan. Add the garlic and turmeric and cook for a few seconds. Stir in the rice and lentils.

2   Add the stock, tomatoes and cinnamon. Season to taste with salt and pepper. Stir once and bring to the boil. Lower the heat, cover and simmer for 20 minutes, until most of the stock is absorbed and the rice and lentils are tender.

3   Stir in the beans, replace the lid and leave to stand for 2–3 minutes to allow the beans to heat through.

4   While the rice is cooking, heat the remaining oil and butter in a frying pan. Add the spring onions and cook for 4–5 minutes, until soft. Lightly beat the eggs with 2 tablespoons of the herbs, then season with salt and pepper.

5   Pour the egg mixture over the spring onions. Stir gently with a spatula over a low heat, drawing the mixture from the sides to the centre as the omelette sets. When almost set, stop stirring and cook for about 30 seconds until golden underneath.

6   Remove the omelette from the pan, roll up and slice into thin strips. Fluff the rice up with a fork and remove the cinnamon stick. Spoon onto serving plates, top with strips of omelette and the remaining chopped herbs. Garnish with sprigs of dill and serve.

1

3

5

Red Lentil Kedgeree with Avocado & Tomatoes

INGREDIENTS

Serves 4

150 g/5 oz basmati rice

150 g/5 oz red lentils

15 g/½ oz butter

1 tbsp sunflower oil

1 medium onion, peeled and chopped

1 tsp ground cumin

4 cardamom pods, bruised

1 bay leaf

450 ml/¾ pint vegetable stock

1 ripe avocado, peeled, stoned
  and diced

1 tbsp lemon juice

4 plum tomatoes, peeled and diced

2 tbsp freshly chopped coriander

salt and freshly ground black pepper

lemon or lime slices, to garnish

TASTY TIP

Although basmati rice and red lentils do not usually need to be pre-soaked, it improves the results of this recipe: the rice will cook to very light, fluffy separate grains and the lentils will just begin to break down giving the dish a creamier texture.

1 Put the rice and lentils in a sieve and rinse under cold running water. Tip into a bowl, then pour over enough cold water to cover and leave to soak for 10 minutes.

2 Heat the butter and oil in a saucepan. Add the sliced onion and cook gently, stirring occasionally, for 10 minutes until softened. Stir in the cumin, cardamon pods and bay leaf and cook for a further minute, stirring all the time.

3 Drain the rice and lentils, rinse again and add to the onions in the saucepan. Stir in the vegetable stock and bring to the boil. Reduce the heat, cover the saucepan and simmer for 15 minutes, or until the rice and lentils are tender.

4 Place the diced avocado in a bowl and toss with the lemon juice. Stir in the tomatoes and chopped coriander. Season to taste with salt and pepper.

5 Fluff up the rice with a fork, spoon into a warmed serving dish and spoon the avocado mixture on top. Garnish with lemon or lime slices and serve.

2

3

4

Aduki Bean & Rice Burgers

INGREDIENTS

Serves 4

2½ tbsp sunflower oil

1 medium onion, peeled and very
  finely chopped

1 garlic clove, peeled and crushed

1 tsp curry paste

225 g/8 oz basmati rice

400 g can aduki beans,
  drained and rinsed

225 ml/8 fl oz vegetable stock

125 g/4 oz firm tofu, crumbled

1 tsp garam masala

2 tbsp freshly chopped coriander

salt and freshly ground black pepper

For the carrot raita:

2 large carrots, peeled and grated

½ cucumber, cut into tiny cubes

150 ml/¼ pint Greek yogurt

To serve:

wholemeal baps

tomato slices

lettuce leaves

1 Heat 1 tablespoon of the oil in a saucepan and gently cook the onion for 10 minutes until soft. Add the garlic and curry paste and cook for a few more seconds. Stir in the rice and beans.

2 Pour in the stock, bring to the boil and simmer for 12 minutes, or until all the stock has been absorbed – do not lift the lid for the first 10 minutes of cooking. Reserve.

3 Lightly mash the tofu. Add to the rice mixture with the garam masala, coriander, salt and pepper. Mix.

4 Divide the mixture into eight and shape into burgers. Chill in the refrigerator for 30 minutes.

5 Meanwhile, make the raita. Mix together the carrots, cucumber and Greek yogurt. Spoon into a small bowl and chill in the refrigerator until ready to serve.

6 Heat the remaining oil in a large frying pan. Fry the burgers, in batches if necessary, for 4–5 minutes on each side, or until lightly browned. Serve in the baps with tomato slices and lettuce. Accompany with the raita.

3

4

5

Venetian–style Vegetables & Beans

INGREDIENTS

Serves 4

250 g/9 oz dried pinto beans
3 sprigs of fresh parsley
1 sprig of fresh rosemary
2 tbsp olive oil
200 g can chopped tomatoes
2 shallots, peeled

For the vegetable mixture:

1 large red onion, peeled
1 large white onion, peeled
1 medium carrot, peeled
2 sticks celery, trimmed
3 tbsp olive oil
3 bay leaves
1 tsp caster sugar
3 tbsp red wine vinegar
salt and freshly ground black pepper

HELPFUL HINT

If time is short, put the beans into a large saucepan and cover with cold water. Bring to the boil and boil rapidly for 10 minutes. Turn off the heat and leave to stand for 2 hours. Drain well and cover with fresh water. Cook as above.

1 Put the beans in a bowl, cover with plenty of cold water and leave to soak for at least 8 hours, or overnight.

2 Drain and rinse the beans. Put in a large saucepan with 1.1 litres/ 2 pints cold water. Tie the parsley and rosemary in muslin and add to the beans with the olive oil. Boil rapidly for 10 minutes, then lower the heat and simmer for 20 minutes with the saucepan half-covered. Stir in the tomatoes and shallots and simmer for a further 10–15 minutes, or until the beans are cooked.

3 Meanwhile, slice the red and white onion into rings and then finely dice the carrot and celery. Heat the olive oil in a saucepan and cook the onions over a very low heat for about 10 minutes. Add the carrot, celery and bay leaves to the saucepan and cook for a further 10 minutes, stirring frequently, until the vegetables are tender. Sprinkle with sugar, stir and cook for 1 minute.

4 Stir in the vinegar. Cook for 1 minute, then remove the saucepan from the heat. Drain the beans through a fine sieve, discarding all the herbs, then add the beans to the onion mixture and season well with salt and pepper. Mix gently, then tip the beans into a large serving bowl. Leave to cool, then serve at room temperature.

2

2

3

Roast Butternut Squash Risotto

INGREDIENTS

Serves 4

1 medium butternut squash
2 tbsp olive oil
1 garlic bulb, cloves separated,
  but unpeeled
15 g/½ oz unsalted butter
275 g/10 oz Arborio rice
large pinch of saffron strands
150 ml/¼ pint dry white wine
1 litre/1¾ pints vegetable stock
1 tbsp freshly chopped parsley
1 tbsp freshly chopped oregano
50 g/2 oz Parmesan cheese,
  finely grated
salt and freshly ground black pepper
sprigs of fresh oregano, to garnish
extra Parmesan cheese, to serve

HELPFUL HINT

It is important to keep the stock simmering alongside the risotto because this ensures that the cooking process is not interrupted.

1. Preheat the oven to 190°C/375°F/Gas Mark 5. Cut the butternut squash in half, thickly peel, then scoop out the seeds and discard. Cut the flesh into 2 cm/¾ inch cubes.

2. Pour the oil into a large roasting tin and heat in the preheated oven for 5 minutes. Add the butternut squash and garlic cloves. Turn in the oil to coat, then roast in the oven for about 25–30 minutes, or until golden brown and very tender, turning the vegetables halfway through cooking time.

3. Melt the butter in a large saucepan. Add the rice and stir over a high heat for a few seconds. Add the saffron and the wine and bubble fiercely until almost totally reduced, stirring frequently. At the same time heat the stock in a separate saucepan and keep at a steady simmer.

4. Reduce the heat under the rice to low. Add a ladleful of stock to the saucepan and simmer, stirring, until absorbed. Continue adding the stock in this way until the rice is tender. This will take about 20 minutes and it may not be necessary to add all the stock.

5. Turn off the heat, stir in the herbs, Parmesan cheese and seasoning. Cover and leave to stand for 2–3 minutes. Quickly remove the skins from the roasted garlic. Add to the risotto with the butternut squash and mix gently. Garnish with sprigs of oregano and serve immediately with Parmesan cheese.

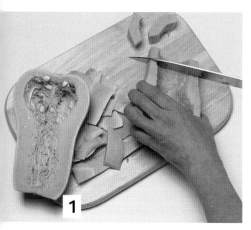

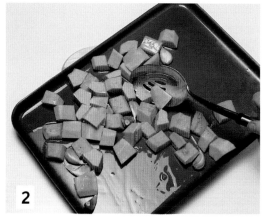

Wild Rice Dolmades

INGREDIENTS

Serves 4-6

6 tbsp olive oil

25 g/1 oz pine nuts

175 g/6 oz mushrooms, wiped
  and finely chopped

4 spring onions, trimmed and
  finely chopped

1 garlic clove, peeled and crushed

50 g/2 oz cooked wild rice

2 tsp freshly chopped dill

2 tsp freshly chopped mint

salt and freshly ground black pepper

16–24 prepared medium vine leaves

about 300 ml/½ pint
  vegetable stock

To garnish:

lemon wedges

sprigs of fresh dill

HELPFUL HINT

Fresh vine leaves are available in early summer and should be blanched for 2–3 minutes in boiling water. Vine leaves preserved in brine can be found all year round in supermarkets – soak in warm water for 20 minutes before using.

1 Heat 1 tbsp of the oil in a frying pan and gently cook the pine nuts for 2–3 minutes, stirring frequently, until golden. Remove from the pan and reserve.

2 Add 1½ tablespoons of oil to the pan and gently cook the mushrooms, spring onions and garlic for 7–8 minutes until very soft. Stir in the rice, herbs, salt and pepper.

3 Put a heaped teaspoon of stuffing in the centre of each leaf. If the leaves are small, put two together, overlapping slightly. Fold over the stalk end, then the sides and roll up to make a neat parcel. Continue until all the stuffing is used.

4 Arrange the stuffed vine leaves close together seam-side down in a large saucepan, drizzling each with a little of the remaining oil – there will be several layers. Pour over just enough stock to cover.

5 Put an inverted plate over the dolmades to stop them unrolling during cooking. Bring to the boil, then simmer very gently for 3 minutes. Cool in the saucepan.

6 Transfer the dolmades to a serving dish. Cover and chill in the refrigerator before serving. Sprinkle with the pine nuts and garnish with lemon and dill. Serve.

2

3

4

Broad Bean & Artichoke Risotto

INGREDIENTS

Serves 4

275 g/10 oz frozen broad beans
400 g can artichoke hearts, drained
1 tbsp sunflower oil
150 ml/¼ pint dry white wine
900 ml/1½ pints vegetable stock
25 g/1 oz butter
1 onion, peeled and finely chopped
200 g/7 oz Arborio rice
finely grated rind and juice of 1 lemon
50 g/2 oz Parmesan cheese, grated
salt and freshly ground black pepper
freshly grated Parmesan cheese,
  to serve

1 Cook the beans in a saucepan of lightly salted boiling water for 4–5 minutes, or until just tender. Drain and plunge into cold water. Peel off the tough outer skins, if liked. Pat the artichokes dry on absorbent kitchen paper and cut each in half lengthways through the stem end. Cut each half into three wedges.

2 Heat the oil in a large saucepan and cook the artichokes for 4–5 minutes, turning occasionally, until they are lightly browned. Remove and reserve. Bring the wine and stock to the boil in a separate frying pan. Keep them barely simmering while making the risotto.

3 Melt the butter in a large frying pan, add the onion and cook for 5 minutes until beginning to soften. Add the rice and cook for 1 minute, stirring. Pour in a ladleful of the hot wine and stock, simmer gently, stirring frequently, until the stock is absorbed. Continue to add the stock in this way for 20–25 minutes, until the rice is just tender; the risotto should look creamy and soft.

4 Add the broad beans, artichokes, and lemon rind and juice. Gently mix in, cover and leave to warm through for 1–2 minutes. Stir in the Parmesan cheese and season to taste with salt and pepper. Serve sprinkled with extra Parmesan cheese.

HELPFUL HINT

If using fresh broad beans, buy about 700 g/1½ lb in their pods. Young fresh beans do not need to be skinned.

Wild Mushroom Risotto

INGREDIENTS

Serves 4

15 g/½ oz dried porcini
1.1 litres/2 pints vegetable stock
75 g/3 oz butter
1 tbsp olive oil
1 onion, peeled and chopped
2–4 garlic cloves, peeled and chopped
1–2 red chillies, deseeded
  and chopped
225 g/8 oz wild mushrooms, wiped
  and halved, if large
125 g/4 oz button mushrooms,
  wiped and sliced
350 g/12 oz Arborio rice
175 g/6 oz large cooked prawns,
  peeled (optional)
150 ml/¼ pint white wine
salt and freshly ground black pepper
1 tbsp lemon zest
1 tbsp freshly snipped chives
2 tbsp freshly chopped parsley

1   Soak the porcini in 300 ml/½ pint of very hot, but not boiling water for 30 minutes. Drain, reserving the mushrooms and soaking liquid. Pour the stock into a saucepan, and bring to the boil, then reduce the heat to keep it simmering.

2   Melt the butter and oil in a large, deep frying pan, add the onion, garlic and chillies and cook gently for 5 minutes. Add the wild and button mushrooms with the drained porcini, and continue to cook for 4–5 minutes, stirring frequently.

3   Stir in the rice and cook for 1 minute. Strain the reserved soaking liquid and stir into the rice with a little of the hot stock. Cook gently, stirring frequently, until the liquid is absorbed. Continue to add most of the stock, a ladleful at a time, cooking after each addition, until the rice is tender and the risotto looks creamy.

4   Add the prawns (if using) and wine along with the last additions of stock. When the prawns are hot and all the liquid is absorbed, season to taste with salt and pepper. Remove from the heat and stir in the lemon zest, chives and parsley, reserving some for the garnish. Garnish and serve.

1

4

4

Warm Noodle Salad with Sesame & Peanut Dressing

INGREDIENTS

Serves 4-6

125 g/4 oz smooth peanut butter
6 tbsp sesame oil
3 tbsp light soy sauce
2 tbsp red wine vinegar
1 tbsp freshly grated root ginger
2 tbsp double cream
250 g pack Chinese fine egg noodles
125 g/4 oz beansprouts
225 g/8 oz baby sweetcorn
125 g/4 oz carrots, peeled and
  cut into matchsticks
125 g/4 oz mangetout
125 g/4 oz cucumber,
  cut into thin strips
3 spring onions, trimmed and
  finely shredded

FOOD FACT

There are two types of sesame oil –
one light and pale and the other
dark and rich. The latter can be
overpowering in large quantities, so
use the light version for this recipe.

1 Place the peanut butter, 4 tablespoons of the sesame oil, the soy sauce, vinegar and ginger in a food processor. Blend until smooth, then stir in 75 ml/3 fl oz hot water and blend again. Pour in the cream and blend briefly until smooth. Pour the dressing into a jug and reserve.

2 Bring a saucepan of lightly salted water to the boil, add the noodles and beansprouts and cook for 4 minutes or according to the packet instructions. Drain, rinse under cold running water and drain again. Stir in the remaining sesame oil and keep warm.

3 Bring a saucepan of lightly salted water to the boil and add the baby sweetcorn, carrots and mangetout and cook for 3–4 minutes, or until just tender but still crisp. Drain and cut the mangetout in half. Slice the baby sweetcorn (if very large) into 2–3 pieces and arrange on a warmed serving dish with the noodles. Add the cucumber strips and spring onions. Spoon over a little of the dressing and serve immediately with the remaining dressing.

2

3

4

Spicy Cucumber Stir Fry

INGREDIENTS

Serves 4

25 g/1 oz black soya beans, soaked in
   cold water overnight
1½ cucumbers
2 tsp salt
1 tbsp groundnut oil
½ tsp mild chilli powder
4 garlic cloves, peeled and crushed
5 tbsp vegetable stock
1 tsp sesame oil
1 tbsp freshly chopped parsley,
   to garnish

FOOD FACT

Black soya beans are small oval beans that are referred to as 'meat of the earth' in China, where they were once considered sacred. Soya beans are the only pulse that contains all eight essential amino acids, so they are an excellent source of protein. They are extremely dense and need to be soaked for at least 5 hours before cooking.

1 Rinse the soaked beans thoroughly, then drain. Place in a saucepan, cover with cold water and bring to the boil, skimming off any scum that rises to the surface. Boil for 10 minutes, then reduce the heat and simmer for 1–1½ hours. Drain and reserve.

2 Peel the cucumbers, slice lengthways and remove the seeds. Cut into 2.5 cm/1 inch slices and place in a colander over a bowl. Sprinkle the salt over the cucumber and leave for 30 minutes. Rinse thoroughly in cold water, drain and pat dry with absorbent kitchen paper.

3 Heat a wok or large frying pan, add the oil and when hot, add the chilli powder, garlic and black beans and stir-fry for 30 seconds. Add the cucumber and stir-fry for 20 seconds.

4 Pour the stock into the wok and cook for 3–4 minutes, or until the cucumber is very tender. The liquid will have evaporated at this stage. Remove from the heat and stir in the sesame oil. Turn into a warmed serving dish, garnish with chopped parsley and serve immediately.

1

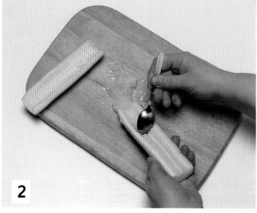
2

3

Chinese Egg Fried Rice

INGREDIENTS

Serves 4

250 g/9 oz long-grain rice
1 tbsp dark sesame oil
2 large eggs
1 tbsp sunflower oil
2 garlic cloves, peeled and crushed
2.5 cm/1 inch piece fresh root ginger, peeled and grated
1 carrot, peeled and cut into matchsticks
125 g/4 oz mangetout, halved
220 g can water chestnuts, drained and halved
1 yellow pepper, deseeded and diced
4 spring onions, trimmed and finely shredded
2 tbsp light soy sauce
½ tsp paprika
salt and freshly ground black pepper

1 Bring a saucepan of lightly salted water to the boil, add the rice and cook for 15 minutes or according to the packet instructions. Drain and leave to cool.

2 Heat a wok or large frying pan and add the sesame oil. Beat the eggs in a small bowl and pour into the hot wok. Using a fork, draw the egg in from the sides of the pan to the centre until it sets, then turn over and cook the other side. When set and golden turn out on to a board. Leave to cool, then cut into very thin strips.

3 Wipe the wok clean with absorbent kitchen paper, return to the heat and add the sunflower oil. When hot add the garlic and ginger and stir-fry for 30 seconds. Add the remaining vegetables and continue to stir-fry for 3–4 minutes, or until tender but still crisp.

4 Stir the reserved cooked rice into the wok with the soy sauce and paprika and season to taste with salt and pepper. Fold in the cooked egg strips and heat through. Tip into a warmed serving dish and serve immediately.

Vegetable Tempura

INGREDIENTS

Serves 4-6

125 g/4 oz rice flour
75 g/3 oz plain flour
4 tsp baking powder
1 tbsp dried mustard powder
2 tsp semolina
salt and freshly ground black pepper
300 ml/½ pint groundnut oil
125 g/4 oz courgette, trimmed
  and thickly sliced
125 g/4 oz mangetout
125 g/4 oz baby sweetcorn
4 small red onions, peeled
  and quartered
1 large red pepper, deseeded and cut
  into 2.5 cm/1 inch wide strips
light soy sauce, to serve

HELPFUL HINT

The batter for these deep-fried vegetable fritters should be very thin. When making take care not to overmix; the batter should be slightly lumpy. Deep-fry a few at a time, or the temperature of the oil will drop and the fritters will not be crisp.

1 Sift the rice flour and the plain flour into a large bowl, then sift in the baking powder and dried mustard powder.

2 Stir the semolina into the flour mixture and season to taste with salt and pepper. Gradually beat in 300 ml/½ pint cold water to produce a thin coating batter. Leave to stand at room temperature for 30 minutes.

3 Heat a wok or large frying pan, add the oil and heat to 180°C/350°F. Working in batches and using a slotted spoon, dip the vegetables in the batter until well coated, then drop them carefully into the hot oil. Cook each batch for 2–3 minutes or until golden. Drain on absorbent kitchen paper and keep warm while cooking the remaining batches.

4 Transfer the vegetables to a warmed serving platter and serve immediately with the light soy sauce to use as a dipping sauce.

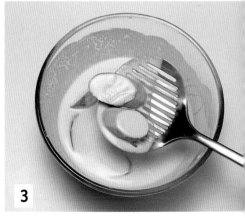

Thai–style Cauliflower & Potato Curry

INGREDIENTS

Serves 4

450 g/1 lb new potatoes, peeled and
   halved or quartered
350 g/12 oz cauliflower florets
3 garlic cloves, peeled and crushed
1 onion, peeled and finely chopped
40 g/1½ oz ground almonds
1 tsp ground coriander
½ tsp ground cumin
½ tsp turmeric
3 tbsp groundnut oil
salt and freshly ground black pepper
50 g/2 oz creamed coconut,
   broken into small pieces
200 ml/7 fl oz vegetable stock
1 tbsp mango chutney
sprigs of fresh coriander, to garnish
freshly cooked long-grain rice,
   to serve

HELPFUL HINT

Mildly flavoured vegetables absorb the taste and colour of spices in this dish. Take care not to overcook the cauliflower; it should be only just tender for this dish. Broccoli florets would make a good alternative.

1 Bring a saucepan of lightly salted water to the boil, add the potatoes and cook for 15 minutes or until just tender. Drain and leave to cool. Boil the cauliflower for 2 minutes, then drain and refresh under cold running water. Drain again and reserve.

2 Meanwhile, blend the garlic, onion, ground almonds and spices with 2 tablespoons of the oil and salt and pepper to taste in a food processor until a smooth paste is formed. Heat a wok, add the remaining oil and when hot, add the spice paste and cook for 3–4 minutes, stirring continuously.

3 Dissolve the creamed coconut in 6 tablespoons of boiling water and add to the wok. Pour in the stock, cook for 2–3 minutes, then stir in the cooked potatoes and cauliflower.

4 Stir in the mango chutney and heat through for 3–4 minutes or until piping hot. Tip into a warmed serving dish, garnish with sprigs of fresh coriander and serve immediately with freshly cooked rice.

2

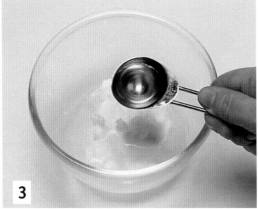

3

3

Coconut–baked Courgettes

INGREDIENTS

Serves 4

3 tbsp groundnut oil
1 onion, peeled and finely sliced
4 garlic cloves, peeled and crushed
½ tsp chilli powder
1 tsp ground coriander
6–8 tbsp dessicated coconut
1 tbsp tomato purée
700 g/1½ lb courgettes,
  thinly sliced
freshly chopped parsley, to garnish

HELPFUL HINT

Because coconut is high in fat, desiccated coconut has a relatively short shelf-life. Unless you use it in large quantities, buy it in small packets, checking the sell-by date. Once opened, desiccated coconut should be used within 2 months. You can also buy it from Asian grocers, but as there is often no sell-by date, smell the contents; it is easy to detect rancid coconut.

1 Preheat the oven to 180°C/350°F/Gas Mark 4, 10 minutes before cooking. Lightly oil a 1.4 litre/2 ½ pint ovenproof gratin dish. Heat a wok, add the oil and when hot, add the onion and stir-fry for 2–3 minutes or until softened. Add the garlic, chilli powder and coriander and stir-fry for 1–2 minutes.

2 Pour 300 ml/½ pint cold water into the wok and bring to the boil. Add the coconut and tomato purée and simmer for 3–4 minutes; most of the water will evaporate at this stage. Spoon 4 tablespoons of the spice and coconut mixture into a small bowl and reserve.

3 Stir the courgettes into the remaining spice and coconut mixture, coating well. Spoon the courgettes into the oiled gratin dish and sprinkle the reserved spice and coconut mixture evenly over the top. Bake, uncovered, in the preheated oven for 15–20 minutes, or until golden. Garnish with chopped parsley and serve immediately.

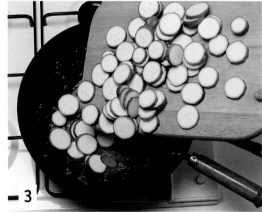

Cooked Vegetable Salad with Satay Sauce

INGREDIENTS

Serves 4

125 ml/4 fl oz groundnut oil
225 g/8 oz unsalted peanuts
1 onion, peeled and finely chopped
1 garlic clove, peeled and crushed
½ tsp chilli powder
1 tsp ground coriander
½ tsp ground cumin
½ tsp sugar
1 tbsp dark soy sauce
2 tbsp fresh lemon juice
2 tbsp light olive oil
salt and freshly ground black pepper
125 g/4 oz French green beans,
    trimmed and halved
125 g/4 oz carrots
125 g/4 oz cauliflower florets
125 g/4 oz broccoli florets
125 g/4 oz Chinese leaves or pak
    choi, trimmed and shredded
125 g/4 oz beansprouts
1 tbsp sesame oil

To garnish:

sprigs of fresh watercress
cucumber, cut into slivers

1 Heat a wok, add the oil, and when hot, add the peanuts and stir-fry for 3–4 minutes. Drain on absorbent kitchen paper and leave to cool. Blend in a food processor to a fine powder.

2 Place the onion and garlic, with the spices, sugar, soy sauce, lemon juice and olive oil in a food processor. Season to taste with salt and pepper, then process into a paste. Transfer to a wok and stir-fry for 3–4 minutes.

3 Stir 600 ml/1 pint hot water into the paste and bring to the boil. Add the ground peanuts and simmer gently for 5–6 minutes or until the mixture thickens. Reserve the satay sauce.

4 Cook in batches in lightly salted boiling water. Cook the French beans, carrots, cauliflower and broccoli for 3–4 minutes, and the Chinese leaves or pak choi and beansprouts for 2 minutes. Drain each batch, drizzle over the sesame oil and arrange on a large warmed serving dish. Garnish with watercress sprigs and cucumber. Serve with the satay sauce.

1

2

3

Mixed Vegetable Stir Fry

INGREDIENTS

Serves 4

2 tbsp groundnut oil

4 garlic cloves, peeled and finely sliced

2.5 cm/1 inch piece fresh root ginger, peeled and finely sliced

75 g/3 oz broccoli florets

50 g/2 oz mangetout, trimmed

75 g/3 oz carrots, peeled and cut into matchsticks

1 green pepper, deseeded and cut into strips

1 red pepper, deseeded and cut into strips

1 tbsp soy sauce

1 tbsp hoisin sauce

1 tsp sugar

salt and freshly ground black pepper

4 spring onions, trimmed and shredded, to garnish

FOOD FACT

Hoisin sauce is a thick, dark brownish red sauce, made by blending soya beans with sugar, vinegar and spices. It has a spicy, sweetish taste and is often used in southern Chinese cooking.

1 Heat a wok, add the oil and when hot, add the garlic and ginger slices and stir-fry for 1 minute.

2 Add the broccoli florets to the wok, stir-fry for 1 minute, then add the mangetout, carrots and the green and red peppers and stir-fry for a further 3–4 minutes, or until tender but still crisp.

3 Blend the soy sauce, hoisin sauce and sugar in a small bowl. Stir well, season to taste with salt and pepper and pour into the wok.

4 Transfer the vegetables to a warmed serving dish. Garnish with shredded spring onions and serve immediately.

1

2

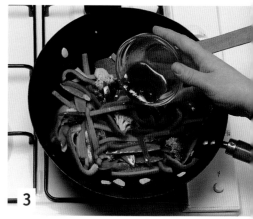

3

Thai Stuffed Eggs with Spinach & Sesame Seeds

INGREDIENTS

Makes 8

4 large eggs
salt and freshly ground black pepper
225 g/8 oz baby spinach
2 garlic cloves, peeled and crushed
1 tbsp spring onions, trimmed
   and finely chopped
1 tbsp sesame seeds
75 g/3 oz plain flour
1 tbsp light olive oil
300 ml/½ pint vegetable oil
   for frying

To garnish:
sliced red chilli
snipped fresh chives

HELPFUL HINT

Eggs are often stuffed with a combination of pork and crabmeat, but this vegetarian version makes a delicious alternative. They can be made up to 24 hours ahead of serving.

1 Bring a small saucepan of water to the boil, add the eggs, bring back to the boil and cook for 6–7 minutes. Plunge into cold water, then shell and cut in half lengthways. Using a teaspoon, remove the yolks and place in a bowl. Reserve the whites.

2 Place 1 teaspoon of water and ½ teaspoon of salt in a saucepan, add the spinach and cook until tender and wilted. Drain, squeeze out the excess moisture and chop. Mix with the egg yolk, then stir in the garlic, spring onions and sesame seeds. Season to taste with salt and pepper. Fill the egg shells with the mixture, smoothing into a mound.

3 Place the flour in a bowl with the olive oil, a large pinch of salt and 125 ml/4 fl oz warm water. Beat together to make a completely smooth batter.

4 Heat a wok, add the vegetable oil and heat to 180°C/350°F. Dip the stuffed eggs in the batter, allowing any excess batter to drip back into the bowl, and deep-fry in batches for 3–4 minutes or until golden brown. Place the eggs in the wok, filled-side down first, then turn over to finish cooking. Remove from the wok with a slotted spoon and drain on absorbent kitchen paper. Serve hot or cold garnished with snipped chives and chilli rings.

1

2

4

Savoury Wontons

INGREDIENTS

Makes 15

125 g/4 oz filo pastry or wonton skins
15 whole chive leaves
225 g/8 oz spinach
25 g/1 oz butter
½ tsp salt
225 g/8 oz mushrooms,
   wiped and roughly chopped
1 garlic clove, peeled and crushed
1–2 tbsp dark soy sauce
2.5 cm/1 inch piece fresh root ginger,
   peeled and grated
salt and freshly ground black pepper
1 small egg, beaten
300 ml/½ pint groundnut oil
   for deep-frying

To garnish:

spring onion curls
radish roses

HELPFUL HINT

It is important to cover the filo pastry squares or wonton skins you are not immediately working with in clingfilm, to prevent them from drying out.

1 Cut the filo pastry or wonton skins into 12.5 cm/5 inch squares, stack and cover with clingfilm. Chill in the refrigerator while preparing the filling. Blanch the chive leaves in boiling water for 1 minute, drain and reserve.

2 Melt the butter in a saucepan, add the spinach and salt and cook for 2–3 minutes or until wilted. Add the mushrooms and garlic and cook for 2–3 minutes or until tender.

3 Transfer the spinach and mushroom mixture to a bowl. Stir in the soy sauce and ginger. Season to taste with salt and pepper.

4 Place a small spoonful of the spinach and mushroom mixture on to a pastry or wonton square and brush the edges with beaten egg. Gather up the four corners to make a little bag and tie with a chive leaf. Make up the remainder of the wontons.

5 Heat a wok, add the oil and heat to 180°C/350°F. Deep-fry the wontons in batches for 2–3 minutes, or until golden and crisp. Drain on absorbent kitchen paper and serve immediately, garnished with spring onion curls and radish roses.

2

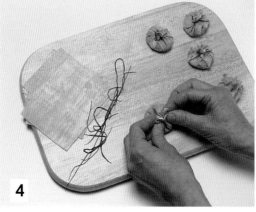

4

5

Corn Fritters with Hot & Spicy Relish

INGREDIENTS

Makes 16-20

For the spicy relish:

3 tbsp sunflower oil
1 onion, peeled and very finely chopped
¼ tsp dried crushed chillies
2 garlic cloves, peeled and crushed
2 tbsp plum sauce

325 g can sweetcorn kernels, drained
1 onion, peeled and very finely chopped
1 spring onion, trimmed and very
 finely chopped
½ tsp chilli powder
1 tsp ground coriander
4 tbsp plain flour
1 tsp baking powder
1 medium egg
salt and freshly ground black pepper
300 ml/½ pint groundnut oil
sprigs of fresh coriander, to garnish

1 First make the relish. Heat a wok, add the sunflower oil and when hot, add the onion and stir-fry for 3–4 minutes or until softened. Add the chillies and garlic, stir-fry for 1 minute, then leave to cool slightly. Stir in the plum sauce, transfer to a food processor and blend until it is the consistency of chutney. Reserve.

2 Place the sweetcorn into a food processor and blend briefly until just mashed. Transfer to a bowl with the onions, chilli powder, coriander, flour, baking powder and egg. Season to taste with salt and pepper and mix together.

3 Heat a wok, add the oil and heat to 180°C/350°F. Working in batches, drop a few spoonfuls of the sweetcorn mixture into the oil and deep-fry for 3–4 minutes, or until golden and crispy, turning occasionally. Using a slotted spoon, remove and drain on absorbent kitchen paper. Arrange on a warmed serving platter, garnish with sprigs of coriander and serve immediately with the relish.

Chinese Leaves with Sweet-&-Sour Sauce

INGREDIENTS

Serves 4

1 head Chinese leaves
200 g pack pak choi
1 tbsp cornflour
1 tbsp soy sauce
2 tbsp brown sugar
3 tbsp red wine vinegar
3 tbsp orange juice
2 tbsp tomato purée
3 tbsp sunflower oil
15 g/½ oz butter
1 tsp salt
2 tbsp toasted sesame seeds

FOOD FACT

Chinese leaves have a mild, delicate, faintly cabbage-like flavour. They have pale, tightly wrapped crinkly leaves and crisp white stems. Because they are now grown in and imported from Spain, Holland and Israel, they are available all year round. They will keep for at least a week in the salad drawer of the refrigerator.

1 Discard any tough outer leaves and stalks from the Chinese leaves and pak choi and wash well. Drain thoroughly and pat dry with absorbent kitchen paper. Shred the Chinese leaves and pak choi lengthways. Reserve.

2 In a small bowl, blend the cornflour with 4 tablespoons of water. Add the soy sauce, sugar, vinegar, orange juice and tomato purée and stir until blended thoroughly.

3 Pour the sauce into a small saucepan and bring to the boil. Simmer gently for 2–3 minutes, or until the sauce is thickened and smooth.

4 Meanwhile, heat a wok or large frying pan and add the sunflower oil and butter. When melted, add the prepared Chinese leaves and pak choi, sprinkle with the salt and stir-fry for 2 minutes. Reduce the heat and cook gently for a further 1–2 minutes or until tender.

5 Transfer the Chinese leaves and pak choi to a warmed serving platter and drizzle over the warm sauce. Sprinkle with the toasted sesame seeds and serve immediately.

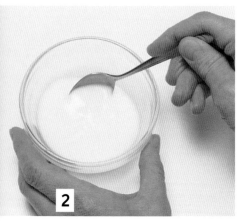

2

3

4

Bean & Cashew Stir Fry

INGREDIENTS

Serves 4

3 tbsp sunflower oil

1 onion, peeled and finely chopped

1 celery stalk, trimmed and chopped

2.5 cm/1 inch piece fresh root ginger,
   peeled and grated

2 garlic cloves, peeled and crushed

1 red chilli, deseeded and
   finely chopped

175 g/6 oz fine French beans,
   trimmed and halved

175 g/6 oz mangetout, sliced
   diagonally into three

75 g/3 oz unsalted cashew nuts

1 tsp brown sugar

125 ml/4 fl oz vegetable stock

2 tbsp dry sherry

1 tbsp light soy sauce

1 tsp red wine vinegar

salt and freshly ground black pepper

freshly chopped coriander, to garnish

1 Heat a wok or large frying pan, add the oil and when hot, add the onion and celery and stir-fry gently for 3–4 minutes or until softened.

2 Add the ginger, garlic and chilli to the wok and stir-fry for 30 seconds. Stir in the French beans and mangetout together with the cashew nuts and continue to stir-fry for 1–2 minutes, or until the nuts are golden brown.

3 Dissolve the sugar in the stock, then blend with the sherry, soy sauce and vinegar. Stir into the bean mixture and bring to the boil. Simmer gently, stirring occasionally for 3–4 minutes, or until the beans and mangetout are tender but still crisp and the sauce has thickened slightly. Season to taste with salt and pepper. Transfer to a warmed serving bowl or spoon on to individual plates. Sprinkle with freshly chopped coriander and serve immediately.

Fried Rice with Bamboo Shoots & Ginger

INGREDIENTS

Serves 4

4 tbsp sunflower oil

1 onion, peeled and finely chopped

225 g/8 oz long-grain rice

3 garlic cloves, peeled and
cut into slivers

2.5 cm/1 inch piece fresh root ginger,
peeled and grated

3 spring onions, trimmed and chopped

450 ml/³/₄ pint vegetable stock

125 g/4 oz button mushrooms,
wiped and halved

75 g/3 oz frozen peas, thawed

2 tbsp light soy sauce

500 g can bamboo shoots, drained
and thinly sliced

salt and freshly ground black pepper

cayenne pepper, to taste

fresh coriander leaves, to garnish

FOOD FACT

Button, cap and flat mushrooms
are actually the same type of
mushroom but in different stages
of maturity. The button mushroom
is the youngest and therefore has
the mildest flavour. Brown-capped
chestnut mushrooms, which look
similar but have a richer, nutty
flavour could also be used here.

1 Heat a wok, add the oil and when hot, add the onion and cook gently for 3–4 minutes, then add the long-grain rice and cook for 3–4 minutes or until golden, stirring frequently.

2 Add the garlic, ginger and chopped spring onions to the wok and stir well. Pour the chicken stock into a small saucepan and bring to the boil. Carefully ladle the hot stock into the wok, stir well, then simmer gently for 10 minutes or until most of the liquid has been absorbed.

3 Stir the button mushrooms, peas and soy sauce into the wok and continue to cook for a further 5 minutes, or until the rice is tender, adding a little extra stock if necessary.

4 Add the bamboo shoots to the wok and carefully stir in. Season to taste with salt, pepper and cayenne pepper. Cook for 2–3 minutes or until heated through. Tip on to a warmed serving dish, garnish with coriander leaves and serve immediately.

1

3

4

Spring Rolls with Mixed Vegetables

INGREDIENTS

Makes 12

2 tbsp sesame oil

125 g/4 oz broccoli florets,
  cut into small pieces

125 g/4 oz carrots, peeled and
  cut into matchsticks

125 g/4 oz courgettes, cut into strips

150 g/5 oz button mushrooms,
  finely chopped

2.5 cm/1 inch piece fresh root ginger,
  peeled and grated

1 garlic clove, peeled and
  finely chopped

4 spring onions, trimmed and
  finely chopped

75 g/3 oz beansprouts

1 tbsp light soy sauce

pinch of cayenne pepper

4 tbsp plain flour

12 sheets filo pastry

300 ml/½ pint groundnut oil

spring onion curls, to garnish

1 Heat a wok, add the sesame oil and when hot, add the broccoli, carrots, courgettes, mushrooms, ginger, garlic and spring onions and stir-fry for 1–2 minutes, or until slightly softened.

2 Turn into a bowl, add the beansprouts, soy sauce and cayenne pepper and mix together. Transfer the vegetables to a colander and drain for 5 minutes. Meanwhile, blend the flour with 2–3 tablespoons of water to form a paste and reserve.

3 Fold a sheet of filo pastry in half and in half again, brushing a little water between each layer. Place a spoonful of the drained vegetable mixture on the pastry. Brush a little of the flour paste along the edges. Turn the edges into the centre, then roll up and seal. Repeat with the rest.

4 Wipe the wok clean, return to the heat, add the oil and heat to 190°C/375°F. Add the spring rolls in batches and deep-fry for 2–3 minutes, or until golden. Drain on absorbent kitchen paper, arrange on a platter, garnish with spring onion curls and serve immediately.

1

2

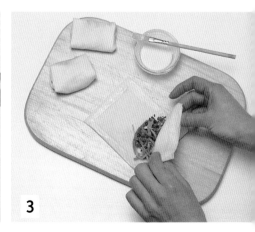

3

Thai Curry with Tofu

INGREDIENTS

Serves 4

750 ml/1¼ pints coconut milk

700 g/1½ lb tofu, drained and cut
  into small cubes

salt and freshly ground black pepper

4 garlic cloves, peeled and chopped

1 large onion, peeled and cut
  into wedges

1 tsp crushed dried chillies

grated rind of 1 lemon

2.5 cm/1 inch piece fresh root ginger,
  peeled and grated

1 tbsp ground coriander

1 tsp ground cumin

1 tsp turmeric

2 tbsp light soy sauce

1 tsp cornflour

Thai fragrant rice, to serve

To garnish:

2 red chillies, deseeded and
  cut into rings

1 tbsp freshly chopped coriander

lemon wedges

1 Pour 600 ml/1 pint of the coconut milk into a saucepan and bring to the boil. Add the tofu, season to taste with salt and pepper and simmer gently for 10 minutes. Using a slotted spoon, remove the tofu and place on a plate. Reserve the coconut milk.

2 Place the garlic, onion, dried chillies, lemon rind, ginger, spices and soy sauce in a blender or food processor and blend until a smooth paste is formed. Pour the remaining 150 ml/¼ pint coconut milk into a clean saucepan and whisk in the spicy paste. Cook, stirring continuously, for 15 minutes, or until the curry sauce is very thick.

3 Gradually whisk the reserved coconut milk into the curry and heat to simmering point. Add the cooked tofu and cook for 5–10 minutes. Blend the cornflour with 1 tablespoon of cold water and stir into the curry. Cook until thickened. Turn into a warmed serving dish and garnish with chilli, lemon wedges and coriander. Serve immediately with Thai fragrant rice.

1

2

3

Chinese Omelette

INGREDIENTS

Serves 1

50 g/2 oz beansprouts

50 g/2 oz carrots, peeled and
   cut into matchsticks

1 cm/½ inch piece fresh root ginger,
   peeled and grated

1 tsp soy sauce

2 large eggs

salt and freshly ground black pepper

1 tbsp dark sesame oil

To serve:

tossed green salad

special fried rice

soy sauce

TASTY TIP

Vary the filling ingredients of this omelette with whatever vegetables you have in your refrigerator. Try sliced spring onions, fine strips of red or green peppers, mangetout halved lengthways, or a few green beans. Cut them into even sizes so that they are all tender at the same time.

1 Lightly rinse the beansprouts, then place in the top of a bamboo steamer with the carrots. Add the grated ginger and soy sauce. Set the steamer over a pan or wok half-filled with gently simmering water and steam for 10 minutes, or until the vegetables are tender but still crisp. Reserve and keep warm.

2 Whisk the eggs in a bowl until frothy and season to taste with salt and pepper. Heat a 20.5 cm/8 inch omelette or frying pan, add the sesame oil and when very hot, pour in the beaten eggs. Whisk the eggs around with a fork, then allow them to cook and start to set. When the top surface starts to bubble, tilt the edges to allow the uncooked egg to run underneath.

3 Spoon the beansprout and carrot mixture over the top of the omelette and allow it to cook a little longer. When it has set, slide the omelette on to a warmed serving dish and carefully roll up. Serve immediately with a tossed green salad, special fried rice and extra soy sauce.

1

2

3

Crispy Pancake Rolls

INGREDIENTS

Makes 8

250 g/9 oz plain flour
pinch of salt
1 medium egg
4 tsp sunflower oil
2 tbsp light olive oil
2 cm/3/4 inch piece fresh root ginger,
    peeled and grated
1 garlic clove, peeled and crushed
225 g/8 oz tofu, drained and
    cut into small cubes
2 tbsp soy sauce
1 tbsp dry sherry
175 g/6 oz button mushrooms,
    wiped and chopped
1 celery stalk, trimmed and
    finely chopped
2 spring onions, trimmed and
    finely chopped
2 tbsp groundnut oil
fresh coriander sprig and sliced
    spring onion, to garnish

1 Sift 225 g/8 oz of the flour with the salt into a large bowl, make a well in the centre and drop in the egg. Beat to form a smooth, thin batter, gradually adding 300 ml/½ pint of water and drawing in the flour from the sides of the bowl. Mix the remaining flour with 1–2 tablespoons of water to make a thick paste. Reserve.

2 Heat a little sunflower oil in a 20.5 cm/8 inch omelette or frying pan and pour in 2 tablespoons of the batter. Cook for 1–2 minutes, flip over and cook for a further 1–2 minutes, or until firm. Slide from the pan and keep warm. Make more pancakes with the remaining batter.

3 Heat a wok or large frying pan, add the olive oil and when hot, add the ginger, garlic and tofu, stir-fry for 30 seconds, then pour in the soy sauce and sherry. Add the mushrooms, celery and spring onions. Stir-fry for 1–2 minutes, then remove from the wok and leave to cool.

4 Place a little filling in the centre of each pancake. Brush the edges with the flour paste, fold in the edges, then roll up into parcels. Heat the groundnut oil to 180°C/350°F in the wok. Fry the pancake rolls for 2–3 minutes or until golden. Serve immediately, garnished with chopped spring onions and a sprig of coriander.

Vegetables in Coconut Milk with Rice Noodles

INGREDIENTS

Serves 4

75 g/3 oz creamed coconut
1 tsp salt
2 tbsp sunflower oil
2 garlic cloves, peeled and
    finely chopped
2 red peppers, deseeded and
    cut into thin strips
2.5 cm/1 inch piece of fresh root
    ginger, peeled and cut into thin strips
125 g/4 oz baby sweetcorn
2 tsp cornflour
2 medium ripe but still firm avocados
1 small Cos lettuce, cut into thick strips
freshly cooked rice noodles, to serve

FOOD FACT

Dried flat rice noodles, rice sticks and stir-fry rice noodles are all made from rice flour and come in varying thicknesses. Check on the packet for cooking instructions; they usually need to be soaked briefly in boiling water, about 2–3 minutes, or slightly longer in hot water.

1 Roughly chop the creamed coconut, place in a bowl with the salt, then pour over 600 ml/1 pint of boiling water. Stir until the coconut has dissolved completely and reserve.

2 Heat a wok or large frying pan, add the oil and when hot, add the chopped garlic, sliced peppers and ginger. Cook for 30 seconds, then cover and cook very gently for 10 minutes or until the peppers are soft.

3 Pour in the reserved coconut milk and bring to the boil. Stir in the baby sweetcorn, cover and simmer for 5 minutes. Blend the cornflour with 2 teaspoons of water, pour into the wok and cook, stirring, for 2 minutes or until thickened slightly.

4 Cut the avocados in half, peel, remove the stone and slice. Add to the wok with the lettuce strips and stir until well mixed and heated through. Serve immediately on a bed of rice noodles.

1

2

4

Thai Fried Noodles

INGREDIENTS

Serves 4

450 g/1 lb tofu
2 tbsp dry sherry
125 g/4 oz medium egg noodles
125 g/4 oz mangetout, halved
3 tbsp groundnut oil
1 onion, peeled and finely sliced
1 garlic clove, peeled and finely sliced
2.5 cm/1 inch piece fresh root ginger,
  peeled and finely sliced
125 g/4 oz beansprouts
1 tbsp Thai fish sauce (optional)
2 tbsp light soy sauce
½ tsp sugar
salt and freshly ground black pepper
½ courgette, cut into matchsticks

To garnish:
2 tbsp roasted peanuts,
  roughly chopped
sprigs of fresh basil

1 Cut the tofu into cubes and place in a bowl. Sprinkle over the sherry and toss to coat. Cover loosely and leave to marinate in the refrigerator for 30 minutes.

2 Bring a large saucepan of lightly salted water to the boil and add the noodles and mangetout. Simmer for 3 minutes or according to the packet instructions, then drain and rinse under cold running water. Leave to drain again.

3 Heat a wok or large frying pan, add the oil and when hot, add the onion and stir-fry for 2–3 minutes. Add the garlic and ginger and stir-fry for 30 seconds. Add the beansprouts and tofu, stir in the Thai fish sauce (if using) and the soy sauce with the sugar and season to taste with salt and pepper.

4 Stir-fry the tofu mixture over a medium heat for 2–3 minutes, then add the courgettes, noodles and mangetout and stir-fry for a further 1–2 minutes. Tip into a warmed serving dish or spoon on to individual plates. Sprinkle with the peanuts, add a sprig of basil and serve immediately.

1

3

4

Stir-fried Greens

INGREDIENTS

Serves 4

450 g/1 lb Chinese leaves
225 g/8 oz pak choi
225 g/8 oz broccoli florets
1 tbsp sesame seeds
1 tbsp groundnut oil
1 tbsp fresh root ginger, peeled and
   finely chopped
3 garlic cloves, peeled
   and finely chopped
2 red chillies, deseeded and
   split in half
50 ml/2 fl oz vegetable stock
2 tbsp Chinese rice wine
1 tbsp dark soy sauce
1 tsp light soy sauce
2 tsp black bean sauce
freshly ground black pepper
2 tsp sugar
1 tsp sesame oil

1   Separate the Chinese leaves and pak choi and wash well. Cut into 2.5 cm/1 inch strips. Separate the broccoli into small florets. Heat a wok or large frying pan, add the sesame seeds and stir-fry for 30 seconds or until browned.

2   Add the oil to the wok and when hot, add the ginger, garlic and chillies and stir-fry for 30 seconds. Add the broccoli and stir-fry for 1 minute. Add the Chinese leaves and pak choi and stir-fry for a further 1 minute.

3   Pour the vegetable stock and Chinese rice wine into the wok with the soy and black bean sauces. Season to taste with pepper and add the sugar. Reduce the heat and simmer for 6–8 minutes, or until the vegetables are tender but still firm to the bite. Tip into a warmed serving dish, removing the chillies if preferred. Drizzle with the sesame oil and serve immediately.

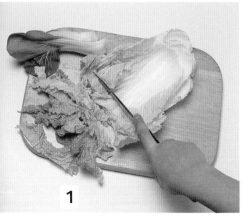

1

2

3

Vegetable Kofta Curry

INGREDIENTS

Serves 6

350 g/12 oz potatoes, peeled and diced
225 g/8 oz carrots, peeled and
  roughly chopped
225 g/8 oz parsnips, peeled and
  roughly chopped
1 medium egg, lightly beaten
75 g/3 oz plain flour, sifted
8 tbsp sunflower oil
2 onions, peeled and sliced
2 garlic cloves, peeled and crushed
2.5 cm/1 inch piece fresh root ginger,
  peeled and grated
2 tbsp garam masala
2 tbsp tomato paste
300 ml/½ pint vegetable stock
250 ml/9 fl oz Greek yogurt
3 tbsp freshly chopped coriander
salt and freshly ground black pepper

FOOD FACT

Greek yogurt is made by straining the excess watery liquid from ordinary yogurt, making it thicker and higher in fat than natural yogurt.

1 Bring a saucepan of lightly salted water to the boil. Add the potatoes, carrots and parsnips. Cover and simmer for 12–15 minutes, or until the vegetables are tender. Drain the vegetables and mash until very smooth. Stir the egg into the vegetable purée, then add the flour and mix to make a stiff paste and reserve.

2 Heat 2 tablespoons of the oil in a wok and gently cook the onions for 10 minutes. Add the garlic and ginger and cook for a further 2–3 minutes, or until very soft and just beginning to colour.

3 Sprinkle the garam masala over the onions and stir in. Add the tomato paste and stock. Bring to the boil, cover and simmer gently for 15 minutes.

4 Meanwhile, heat the remaining oil in a wok or frying pan. Drop in tablespoons of vegetable batter, four or five at a time and fry, turning often, for 3–4 minutes until brown and crisp. Remove with a slotted spoon and drain on absorbent kitchen paper. Keep warm in a low oven while cooking the rest.

5 Stir the yogurt and coriander into the onion sauce. Slowly heat to boiling point and season to taste with salt and pepper. Divide the koftas between warmed serving plates and spoon over the sauce. Serve immediately.

Thai Noodles & Vegetables with Tofu

INGREDIENTS

Serves 4

225 g/8 oz firm tofu
2 tbsp soy sauce
rind of 1 lime, grated
2 lemon grass stalks
1 red chilli
1 litre/1³/₄ pints vegetable stock
2 slices fresh root ginger, peeled
2 garlic cloves, peeled
2 sprigs of fresh coriander
175 g/6 oz dried thread egg noodles
125 g/4 oz shiitake or button
   mushrooms, sliced if large
2 carrots, peeled and
   cut into matchsticks
125 g/4 oz mangetout
125 g/4 oz bok choy or
   other Chinese leaf
1 tbsp freshly
   chopped coriander
salt and freshly ground
   black pepper
coriander sprigs, to garnish

1 Drain the tofu well and cut into cubes. Put into a shallow dish with the soy sauce and lime rind. Stir well to coat and leave to marinate for 30 minutes.

2 Meanwhile, put the lemon grass and chilli on a chopping board and bruise with the side of a large knife, ensuring the blade is pointing away from you. Put the vegetable stock in a large saucepan and add the lemon grass, chilli, ginger, garlic, and coriander. Bring to the boil, cover and simmer gently for 20 minutes.

3 Strain the stock into a clean pan. Return to the boil and add the noodles, tofu and its marinade and the mushrooms. Simmer gently for 4 minutes.

4 Add the carrots, mangetout, bok choy, coriander and simmer for a further 3–4 minutes until the vegetables are just tender. Season to taste with salt and pepper. Garnish with coriander sprigs. Serve immediately.

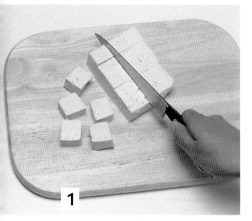
1

2

3

Pad Thai Noodles with Mushrooms

INGREDIENTS

Serves 4

125 g/4 oz flat rice noodles
  or rice vermicelli
1 tbsp vegetable oil
2 garlic cloves, peeled
  and finely chopped
1 medium egg, lightly beaten
225 g/8 oz mixed
  mushrooms, including shiitake,
  oyster, field, brown and
  wild mushrooms
2 tbsp lemon juice
1¹⁄₂ tbsp Thai fish sauce (optional)
¹⁄₂ tsp sugar
¹⁄₂ tsp cayenne pepper
2 spring onions, trimmed and cut
  into 2.5 cm/1 inch pieces
50 g/2 oz fresh beansprouts

To garnish:

chopped roasted peanuts
freshly chopped coriander

1 Cook the noodles according to the packet instructions. Drain well and reserve.

2 Heat a wok or large frying pan and add the oil and garlic. Fry until just golden, then add the egg and stir quickly to break it up.

3 Cook for a few seconds before adding the noodles and mushrooms. Scrape down the sides of the pan to ensure they mix with the egg and garlic.

4 Add the lemon juice, fish sauce (if using), sugar, cayenne pepper, spring onions and half of the beansprouts, stirring quickly all the time.

5 Cook over a high heat for a further 2–3 minutes until everything is heated through.

6 Turn on to a serving plate. Top with the remaining beansprouts. Garnish with the chopped peanuts and coriander and serve immediately.

Vegetable Biryani

INGREDIENTS

Serves 4

2 tbsp vegetable oil, plus a little
   extra for brushing

2 large onions, peeled and thinly
   sliced lengthwise

2 garlic cloves, peeled and
   finely chopped

2.5 cm/1 inch piece fresh root ginger,
   peeled and finely grated

1 small carrot, peeled and
   cut into sticks

1 small parsnip, peeled and diced

1 small sweet potato chunks, peeled
   and diced

1 tbsp medium curry paste

225 g/8 oz basmati rice

4 ripe tomatoes, peeled, deseeded
   and diced

600 ml/1 pint vegetable stock

175 g/6 oz cauliflower florets

50 g/2 oz peas, thawed if frozen

salt and freshly ground black pepper

To garnish:

roasted cashew nuts

raisins

fresh coriander leaves

1 Preheat the oven to 200°C/400°F/Gas Mark 6. Put 1 tablespoon of the vegetable oil in a large bowl with the onions and toss to coat. Lightly brush or spray a non-stick baking sheet with a little more oil. Spread half the onions on the baking sheet and cook at the top of the preheated oven for 25–30 minutes, stirring regularly, until golden and crisp. Remove from the oven and reserve for the garnish.

2 Meanwhile, heat a large flameproof casserole dish over a medium heat and add the remaining oil and onions. Cook for 5–7 minutes until softened and starting to brown. Add a little water if they start to stick. Add the garlic and ginger and cook for another minute, then add the carrot, parsnip and sweet potato. Cook the vegetables for a further 5 minutes.

3 Add the curry paste and stir for a minute until everything is coated, then stir in the rice and tomatoes. After 2 minutes add the stock and stir well. Bring to the boil, cover and simmer over a very gentle heat for about 10 minutes.

4 Add the cauliflower and peas and cook for 8–10 minutes, or until the rice is tender. Season to taste with salt and pepper. Serve garnished with the crispy onions, cashew nuts, raisins and coriander.

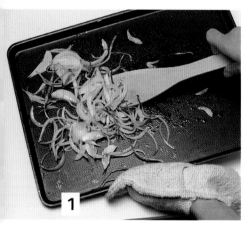
1

2

4

Brown Rice Spiced Pilaf

INGREDIENTS

Serves 4

1 tbsp vegetable oil
1 tbsp blanched almonds,
  flaked or chopped
1 onion, peeled and chopped
1 carrot, peeled and diced
225 g/8 oz flat mushrooms,
  sliced thickly
¼ tsp cinnamon
large pinch dried chilli flakes
50 g/2 oz dried apricots,
  roughly chopped
25 g/1 oz currants
zest of 1 orange
350 g/12 oz brown basmati rice
900 ml/1½ pints vegetable stock
2 tbsp freshly chopped coriander
2 tbsp freshly snipped chives
salt and freshly ground black pepper
snipped chives, to garnish

1 Preheat the oven to 200°C/400°F/Gas Mark 6. Heat the oil in a large flameproof casserole dish and add the almonds. Cook for 1–2 minutes until just browning. Be very careful as the nuts will burn easily.

2 Add the onion and carrot. Cook for 5 minutes until softened and starting to turn brown. Add the mushrooms and cook for a further 5 minutes, stirring often.

3 Add the cinnamon and chilli flakes and cook for about 30 seconds before adding the apricots, currants, orange zest and rice.

4 Stir together well and add the stock. Bring to the boil, cover tightly and transfer to the preheated oven. Cook for 45 minutes until the rice and vegetables are tender.

5 Stir the coriander and chives into the pilaf and season to taste with salt and pepper. Garnish with the extra chives and serve immediately.

2

3

5

Creamy Vegetable Korma

INGREDIENTS

Serves 4-6

2 tbsp ghee or vegetable oil

1 large onion, peeled and chopped

2 garlic cloves, peeled and crushed

2.5 cm/1 inch piece of root ginger, peeled and grated

4 cardamom pods

2 tsp ground coriander

1 tsp ground cumin

1 tsp ground turmeric

finely grated rind and juice of ½ lemon

50 g/2 oz ground almonds

400 ml/14 fl oz vegetable stock

450 g/1 lb potatoes, peeled and diced

450 g/1 lb mixed vegetables, such as cauliflower, carrots and turnip, cut into chunks

150 ml/¼ pint double cream

3 tbsp freshly chopped coriander

salt and freshly ground black pepper

naan bread, to serve

1 Heat the ghee or oil in a large saucepan. Add the onion and cook for 5 minutes. Stir in the garlic and ginger and cook for a further 5 minutes, or until soft and just beginning to colour.

2 Stir in the cardamom, ground coriander, cumin and turmeric. Continue cooking over a low heat for 1 minute, stirring.

3 Stir in the lemon rind and juice and almonds. Blend in the vegetable stock. Slowly bring to the boil, stirring occasionally.

4 Add the potatoes and vegetables. Bring back to the boil, then reduce the heat, cover and simmer for 35–40 minutes, or until the vegetables are just tender. Check after 25 minutes and add a little more stock if needed.

5 Slowly stir in the cream and chopped coriander. Season to taste with salt and pepper. Cook very gently until heated through, but do not boil. Serve immediately with naan bread.

2

4

6

Chinese Salad with Soy & Ginger Dressing

INGREDIENTS

Serves 4

1 head of Chinese cabbage
200 g can water
  chestnuts, drained
6 spring onions, trimmed
4 ripe but firm cherry tomatoes
125 g/4 oz mangetout
125 g/4 oz beansprouts
2 tbsp freshly chopped coriander

For the soy and ginger dressing:

2 tbsp sunflower oil
4 tbsp light soy sauce
2.5 cm/1 inch piece root ginger,
  peeled and finely grated
zest and juice of 1 lemon
salt and freshly ground black pepper
crusty white bread, to serve

1 Rinse and finely shred the Chinese cabbage and place in a serving dish.

2 Slice the water chestnuts into small slivers and cut the spring onions diagonally into 2.5 cm/1 inch lengths, then split lengthwise into thin strips.

3 Cut the tomatoes in half and then slice each half into three wedges and reserve.

4 Simmer the mangetout in boiling water for 2 minutes until beginning to soften, drain and cut in half diagonally.

5 Arrange the water chestnuts, spring onions, mangetout, tomatoes and beansprouts on top of the shredded Chinese cabbage. Garnish with the freshly chopped coriander.

6 Make the dressing by whisking all the ingredients together in a small bowl until mixed thoroughly. Serve with the bread and the salad.

2

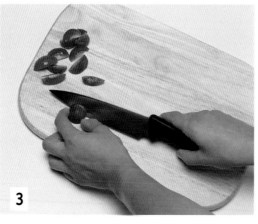

3

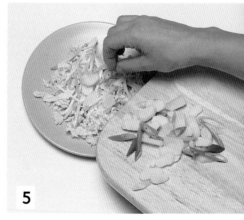

5

Potato Gnocchi with Pesto Sauce

INGREDIENTS

Serves 6

900 g/2 lb floury potatoes
40 g/1½ oz butter
1 medium egg, beaten
225 g/8 oz plain flour
1 tsp salt
freshly ground black pepper
25 g/1 oz Parmesan cheese, shaved
rocket salad, to serve

For the pesto sauce:

50 g/2 oz fresh basil leaves
1 large garlic clove, peeled
2 tbsp pine nuts
125 ml/4 fl oz olive oil
40 g/1½ oz Parmesan cheese, grated

1 Cook the potatoes in their skins in boiling water for 20 minutes, or until tender. Drain and peel. While still warm, push the potatoes through a fine sieve into a bowl. Stir in the butter, egg, 175 g/6 oz of the flour, the salt and pepper.

2 Sift the remaining flour onto a board or work surface and add the potato mixture. Gently knead in enough flour until a soft, slightly sticky dough is formed.

3 With floured hands, break off portions of the dough and roll into 2.5 cm/1 inch thick ropes. Cut into 2 cm/³⁄₄ inch lengths. Lightly press each piece against the inner prongs of a fork. Put on a tray covered with a floured tea towel and chill in the refrigerator for about 30 minutes.

4 To make the pesto sauce, put the basil, garlic, pine nuts and oil in a processor and blend until smooth and creamy. Turn into a bowl and stir in the Parmesan cheese. Season to taste.

5 Cooking in several batches, drop the gnocchi into a saucepan of barely simmering salted water. Cook for 3–4 minutes, or until they float to the surface. Remove with a slotted spoon and keep warm in a covered oiled baking dish in a low oven.

6 Add the gnocchi to the pesto sauce and toss gently to coat. Serve immediately, scattered with the Parmesan cheese and accompanied by a rocket salad.

HELPFUL HINT

Use a vegetable peeler to pare the Parmesan cheese into decorative thin curls.

1

3

5

Fusilli Pasta with Spicy Tomato Salsa

INGREDIENTS

Serves 4

6 large ripe tomatoes

2 tbsp lemon juice

2 tbsp lime juice

grated rind of 1 lime

2 shallots, peeled and finely chopped

2 garlic cloves, peeled
   and finely chopped

1–2 red chillies

1–2 green chillies

450 g/1 lb fresh fusilli pasta

4 tbsp crème fraîche

2 tbsp freshly chopped basil

sprig of oregano, to garnish

FOOD FACT

Pasta is an excellent source of complex carbohydrate and is vital for a healthy lifestyle. Complex carbohydrates are broken down by the body more slowly than simple carbohydrates (contained in cakes, sweets and biscuits) and provide a sustained source of energy.

1 Place the tomatoes in a bowl and cover with boiling water. Allow to stand until the skins start to peel away.

2 Remove the skins from the tomatoes, divide each tomato in four and remove all the seeds. Chop the flesh into small cubes and put in a small pan. Add the lemon and lime juice and the grated lime rind and stir well.

3 Add the chopped shallots and garlic. Remove the seeds carefully from the chillies, chop finely and add to the pan.

4 Bring to the boil and simmer gently for 5–10 minutes until the salsa has thickened slightly.

5 Reserve the salsa to allow the flavours to develop while the pasta is cooking.

6 Bring a large pan of water to the boil and add the pasta. Simmer gently for 3–4 minutes or until the pasta is just tender.

7 Drain the pasta and rinse in boiling water. Top with a large spoonful of salsa and a small spoonful of crème fraîche. Garnish with the chopped basil and oregano and serve immediately.

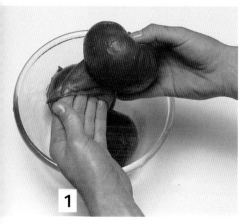

1

3

6

Pasta with Courgettes, Rosemary & Lemon

INGREDIENTS

Serves 4

350 g/12 oz dried pasta shapes,
  e.g. rigatoni
1½ tbsp good quality
  extra virgin olive oil
2 garlic cloves, peeled
  and finely chopped
4 medium courgettes, thinly sliced
1 tbsp freshly chopped rosemary
1 tbsp freshly chopped parsley
zest and juice of 2 lemons
25 g/1 oz pitted black olives,
  roughly chopped
25 g/1 oz pitted green olives,
  roughly chopped
salt and freshly ground black pepper

To garnish:
lemon slices
sprigs of fresh rosemary

TASTY TIP

Look out for patty pan squashes –
small yellow or green squashes,
shaped a little like flying saucers.
They are a good substitute for the
courgettes in this recipe.

1 Bring a large saucepan of salted water to the boil and add the pasta.

2 Return to the boil and cook until 'al dente' or according to the packet instructions.

3 Meanwhile, when the pasta is almost done, heat the oil in a large frying pan and add the garlic.

4 Cook over a medium heat until the garlic just begins to brown. Be careful not to overcook the garlic at this stage or it will become bitter.

5 Add the courgettes, rosemary, parsley and lemon zest and juice. Cook for 3–4 minutes until the courgettes are just tender.

6 Add the olives to the frying pan and stir well. Season to taste with salt and pepper and remove from the heat.

7 Drain the pasta well and add to the frying pan. Stir until thoroughly combined. Garnish with lemon and sprigs of fresh rosemary and serve immediately.

Vegetarian Spaghetti Bolognese

INGREDIENTS

Serves 4

2 tbsp olive oil

1 onion, peeled and finely chopped

1 carrot, peeled and finely chopped

1 celery stick, trimmed and
  finely chopped

225 g/8 oz Quorn mince

150 ml/5 fl oz red wine

300 ml/½ pint vegetable stock

1 tsp mushroom ketchup

4 tbsp tomato purée

350 g/12 oz dried spaghetti

4 tbsp crème fraîche

salt and freshly ground black pepper

1 tbsp freshly chopped parsley

1 Heat the oil in a large saucepan and add the onion, carrot and celery. Cook gently for 10 minutes, adding a little water if necessary, until softened and starting to brown.

2 Add the Quorn mince and cook a further 2–3 minutes before adding the red wine. Increase the heat and simmer gently until nearly all the wine has evaporated.

3 Mix together the vegetable stock and mushroom ketchup and add about half to the Quorn mixture along with the tomato purée. Cover and simmer gently for about 45 minutes, adding the remaining stock as necessary.

4 Meanwhile, bring a large pan of salted water to the boil and add the spaghetti. Cook until 'al dente' or according to the packet instructions. Drain well. Remove the sauce from the heat, add the crème fraîche and season to taste with salt and pepper. Stir in the parsley and serve immediately with the pasta.

HELPFUL HINT

Quorn is a mycroprotein that is high in fibre and low in fat. It is derived from the mushroom family and readily takes on any flavour it is put with. An equivalent amount of soya mince can be used in this recipe, whether dried (follow the packet instructions) or frozen.

Tagliatelle with Broccoli & Sesame

INGREDIENTS

Serves 2

225 g/8 oz broccoli, cut into florets
125 g/4 oz baby corn
175 g/6 oz dried tagliatelle
1½ tbsp tahini paste
1 tbsp dark soy sauce
1 tbsp dark muscovado sugar
1 tbsp red wine vinegar
1 tbsp sunflower oil
1 garlic clove, peeled and
   finely chopped
2.5 cm/1 inch piece fresh root ginger,
   peeled and shredded
½ tsp dried chilli flakes
salt and freshly ground black pepper
1 tbsp toasted sesame seeds
slices of radish, to garnish

1 Bring a large saucepan of salted water to the boil and add the broccoli and corn. Return the water to the boil then remove the vegetables at once using a slotted spoon, reserving the water. Plunge them into cold water and drain well. Dry on kitchen paper and reserve.

2 Return the water to the boil. Add the tagliatelle and cook until 'al dente' or according to the packet instructions. Drain well. Run under cold water until cold, then drain well again.

3 Place the tahini, soy sauce, sugar and vinegar into a bowl. Mix well, then reserve. Heat the oil in a wok or large frying pan over a high heat and add the garlic, ginger and chilli flakes and stir-fry for about 30 seconds. Add the broccoli and baby corn and continue to stir-fry for about 3 minutes.

4 Add the tagliatelle to the wok along with the tahini mixture and stir together for a further 1–2 minutes until heated through. Season to taste with salt and pepper. Sprinkle with sesame seeds, garnish with the radish slices and serve immediately.

FOOD FACT

Tahini is made from ground sesame seeds and is generally available in large supermarkets and Middle Eastern shops. It is most often used in houmous.

1

3

4

Rice & Vegetable Timbale

INGREDIENTS

Serves 6

25 g/1 oz dried white breadcrumbs
3 tbsp olive oil
2 courgettes, sliced
1 small aubergine, cut into
  1 cm/½ inch cubes
175 g/6 oz mushrooms, sliced
1 garlic clove, peeled and crushed
1 tsp balsamic vinegar
1 onion, peeled and finely chopped
25 g/1 oz unsalted butter
400 g/14 oz Arborio rice
about 1.3 litres/2¼ pints boiling
  vegetable stock
2 medium eggs, lightly beaten
25 g/1 oz Parmesan cheese,
  finely grated
2 tbsp freshly chopped basil
salt and freshly ground black pepper

To garnish:
sprig of fresh basil
1 radish, thinly sliced

1 Preheat oven to 190°C/375°F/Gas Mark 5, 10 minutes before cooking. Sprinkle the breadcrumbs over the base and sides of a thickly buttered 20.5 cm/8 inch round, loose-bottomed tin.

2 Heat the olive oil in a large frying pan and gently fry the courgettes, aubergine, mushrooms and garlic for 5 minutes, or until beginning to soften. Stir in the vinegar. Tip the vegetables into a large sieve placed over a bowl to catch the juices.

3 Fry the onion gently in the butter for 10 minutes, until soft. Add the rice and stir for a minute to coat. Add a ladleful of stock and any juices from the vegetables and simmer, stirring, until the rice has absorbed all of the liquid.

4 Continue adding the stock in this way, until the rice is just tender. This should take about 20 minutes. Remove from the heat and leave to cool for 5 minutes. Stir in the eggs, cheese and basil. Season to taste with salt and pepper.

5 Spoon a quarter of the rice into the prepared tin. Top with one-third of the vegetable mixture. Continue layering up in this way, finishing with a layer of rice.

6 Level the top of the layer of rice, gently pressing down the mixture. Cover with a piece of tinfoil. Put on a baking sheet and bake in the preheated oven for 50 minutes, or until firm.

7 Leave the timbale to stand in the tin for 10 minutes, still covered with tinfoil, then turn out on to a warmed serving platter. Garnish with a sprig of fresh basil and slices of radish and serve immediately.

1

2

5

Vegetables Braised in Olive Oil & Lemon

INGREDIENTS

Serves 4

small strip of pared rind and juice
  of ½ lemon
4 tbsp olive oil
1 bay leaf
large sprig of thyme
150 ml/¼ pint water
4 spring onions, trimmed
  and finely chopped
175 g/6 oz baby button mushrooms
175 g/6 oz broccoli, cut into
  small florets
175 g/6 oz cauliflower, cut into
  small florets
1 medium courgette, sliced on
  the diagonal
2 tbsp freshly snipped chives
salt and freshly ground black pepper
lemon zest, to garnish

1 Put the pared lemon rind and juice into a large saucepan. Add the olive oil, bay leaf, thyme and the water. Bring to the boil. Add the spring onions and mushrooms. Top with the broccoli and cauliflower, if possible adding them so that the stalks are submerged in the water and the tops are just above it. Cover and simmer for 3 minutes.

2 Scatter the courgettes on top, so that they are steamed rather than boiled. Cook, covered, for a further 3–4 minutes, until all the vegetables are tender. Using a slotted spoon, transfer the vegetables from the liquid into a warmed serving dish. Increase the heat and boil rapidly for 3–4 minutes, or until the liquid is reduced to about 8 tablespoons. Remove the lemon rind, bay leaf and thyme sprig and discard.

3 Stir the chives into the reduced liquid, season to taste with salt and pepper and pour over the vegetables. Sprinkle with lemon zest and serve immediately.

TASTY TIP

Toast some crusty bread, rub with a garlic clove and drizzle with a little olive oil and top with a spoonful of these vegetables.

Melanzane Parmigiana

INGREDIENTS

Serves 4

900 g/2 lb aubergines
salt and freshly ground black pepper
5 tbsp olive oil
1 red onion, peeled and chopped
$\frac{1}{2}$ tsp mild paprika pepper
150 ml/$\frac{1}{4}$ pint dry red wine
150 ml/$\frac{1}{4}$ pint vegetable stock
400 g can chopped tomatoes
1 tsp tomato purée
1 tbsp freshly chopped oregano
175 g/6 oz mozzarella cheese,
   thinly sliced
40 g/1$\frac{1}{2}$ oz Parmesan cheese,
   coarsely grated
sprig of fresh basil, to garnish

1   Preheat oven to 200°C/400°F/Gas Mark 6, 15 minutes before cooking. Cut the aubergines lengthways into thin slices. Sprinkle with salt and leave to drain in a colander over a bowl for 30 minutes.

2   Meanwhile, heat 1 tablespoon of the olive oil in a saucepan and fry the onion for 10 minutes, until softened. Add the paprika and cook for 1 minute. Stir in the wine, stock, tomatoes and tomato purée. Simmer, uncovered, for 25 minutes, or until fairly thick. Stir in the oregano and season to taste with salt and pepper. Remove from the heat.

3   Rinse the aubergine slices thoroughly under cold water and pat dry on absorbent kitchen paper. Heat 2 tablespoons of the oil in a griddle pan and cook the aubergines in batches, for 3 minutes on each side, until golden. Drain well on absorbent kitchen paper.

4   Pour half of the tomato sauce into the base of a large ovenproof dish. Cover with half the aubergine slices, then top with the mozzarella. Cover with the remaining aubergine slices and pour over the remaining tomato sauce. Sprinkle with the grated Parmesan cheese.

5   Bake in the preheated oven for 30 minutes, or until the aubergines are tender and the sauce is bubbling. Garnish with a sprig of fresh basil and cool for a few minutes before serving.

HELPFUL HINT

Salting the aubergine draws out some of the moisture, so you'll need less oil when frying.

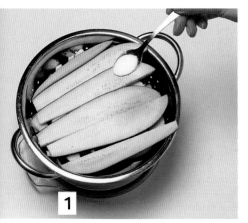
1

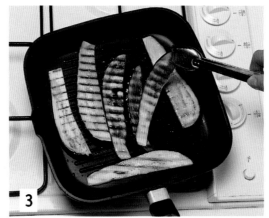
3

4

Stuffed Tomatoes with Grilled Polenta

INGREDIENTS

Serves 4

For the polenta:
300 ml/½ pint vegetable stock
salt and freshly ground black pepper
50 g/2 oz quick-cook polenta
15 g/½ oz butter

For the stuffed tomatoes:
4 large tomatoes
1 tbsp olive oil
1 garlic clove, peeled and crushed
1 bunch spring onions, trimmed and
   finely chopped
2 tbsp freshly chopped parsley
2 tbsp freshly chopped basil
50 g/2 oz fresh white breadcrumbs
snipped chives, to garnish

1 Preheat grill just before cooking. To make the polenta, pour the stock into a saucepan. Add a pinch of salt and bring to the boil. Pour in the polenta in a fine stream, stirring all the time. Simmer for about 15 minutes, or until very thick. Stir in the butter and add a little pepper. Turn the polenta out on to a chopping board and spread to a thickness of just over 1 cm/½ inch. Cool, cover with clingfilm and chill in the refrigerator for 30 minutes.

2 To make the stuffed tomatoes, cut the tomatoes in half then scoop out the seeds and press through a fine sieve to extract the juices. Season the insides of the tomatoes with salt and pepper and reserve.

3 Heat the olive oil in a saucepan and gently fry the garlic and spring onions for 3 minutes. Add the tomatoes' juices and bubble for 3–4 minutes, until most of the liquid has evaporated. Stir in the herbs and a little black pepper with half the breadcrumbs. Spoon into the hollowed out tomatoes and reserve.

4 Cut the polenta into 5 cm/2 inch squares, then cut each in half diagonally to make triangles. Put the triangles on a piece of tinfoil on the grill rack and grill for 4–5 minutes on each side, until golden. Cover and keep warm.

5 Grill the tomatoes under a medium-hot grill for about 4 minutes. Sprinkle with the remaining breadcrumbs and grill for 1–2 minutes, or until the breadcrumbs are golden brown. Garnish with snipped chives and serve immediately with the grilled polenta.

1

3

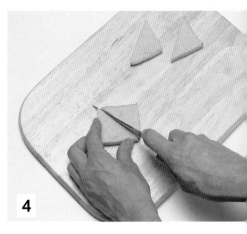

4

Rigatoni with Roasted Beetroot & Rocket

INGREDIENTS

Serves 4

350 g/12 oz raw baby
  beetroot, unpeeled
1 garlic clove, peeled and crushed
$\frac{1}{2}$ tsp finely grated orange rind
1 tbsp orange juice
1 tsp lemon juice
2 tbsp walnut oil
salt and freshly ground black pepper
350 g/12 oz dried fettucini
75 g/3 oz rocket leaves
125 g/4 oz Dolcelatte cheese,
  cut into small cubes

1 Preheat the oven to 150°C/300°F/Gas Mark 2, 10 minutes before cooking. Wrap the beetroot individually in tinfoil and bake for 1–1$\frac{1}{2}$ hours, or until tender. Test by opening one of the parcels and scraping the skin away from the stem end – it should come off very easily.

2 Leave the beetroot until cool enough to handle, then peel and cut each beetroot into 6–8 wedges, depending on the size. Mix the garlic, orange rind and juice, lemon juice, walnut oil and salt and pepper together, then drizzle over the beetroot and toss to coat well.

3 Meanwhile, bring a large saucepan of lightly salted water to the boil. Cook the pasta for 10 minutes, or until 'al dente'.

4 Drain the pasta thoroughly, then add the warm beetroot, rocket leaves and Dolcelatte cheese. Quickly and gently toss together, then divide between serving bowls and serve immediately before the rocket wilts.

HELPFUL HINT

Many large supermarkets sell raw beetroot, but baby beetroot may be more readily available from specialist or ethnic greengrocers. Look for beetroot with the leaves attached. The bulbs should be firm without any soft spots and the leaves should not be wilted.

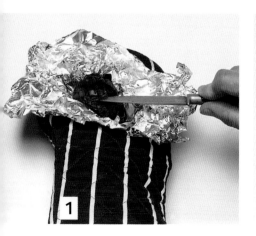
1

2

4

Rice-filled Peppers

INGREDIENTS

Serves 4

8 ripe tomatoes
2 tbsp olive oil
1 onion, peeled and chopped
1 garlic clove, peeled and crushed
½ tsp dark muscovado sugar
125 g/4 oz cooked long-grain rice
50 g/2 oz pine nuts, toasted
1 tbsp freshly chopped oregano
salt and freshly ground black pepper
2 large red peppers
2 large yellow peppers

To serve:

mixed salad
crusty bread

HELPFUL HINT

It may be necessary to take a very thin slice from the bottom of the peppers to enable them to stand on the baking sheet. Be careful not to cut right through.

1 Preheat the oven to 200°C/400°F/Gas Mark 6. Put the tomatoes in a small bowl and pour over boiling water to cover. Leave for 1 minute, then drain. Plunge the tomatoes into cold water to cool, then peel off the skins. Quarter, remove the seeds and chop.

2 Heat the olive oil in a frying pan, and cook the onion gently for 10 minutes, until softened. Add the garlic, chopped tomatoes and sugar.

3 Gently cook the tomato mixture for 10 minutes until thickened. Remove from the heat and stir the rice, pine nuts and oregano into the sauce. Season to taste with salt and pepper.

4 Halve the peppers lengthways, cutting through and leaving the stem on. Remove the seeds and cores, then put the peppers in a lightly oiled roasting tin, cut-side down and cook in the preheated oven for about 10 minutes.

5 Turn the peppers so they are cut side up. Spoon in the filling, then cover with tinfoil. Return to the oven for 15 minutes, or until the peppers are very tender, removing the tinfoil for the last 5 minutes to allow the tops to brown a little.

6 Serve one red pepper half and one yellow pepper half per person with a mixed salad and plenty of warmed, crusty bread.

2

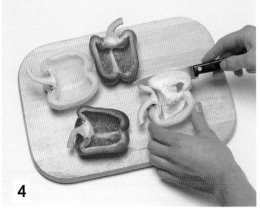

4

5

Pasta with Spicy Red Pepper Sauce

INGREDIENTS

Serves 4

2 red peppers
2 tbsp olive oil
1 onion, peeled and chopped
2 garlic cloves, peeled and crushed
1 red chilli, seeded and finely chopped
200 g/7 oz can chopped tomatoes
finely grated rind and juice of
 ½ lemon
salt and freshly ground black pepper
2–3 tbsp vegetable stock (optional)
400 g/14 oz dried pasta, such as
 tagliatelle, linguine or shells

To garnish:

shaved Parmesan cheese
fresh basil leaves

TASTY TIP

If you prefer a chunkier sauce, do not put the peppers through the food processor but finely chop instead. Add to the saucepan with the onion mixture and carry on from step 4.

1 Preheat grill. Set the whole peppers on the grill rack about 10 cm/ 4 inches away from the heat, then grill, turning frequently, for 10 minutes, until the skins are blackened and blistered.

2 Put the peppers in a plastic bag, and leave until cool enough to handle. Peel off the skin, then halve the peppers and scrape away the seeds. Chop the pepper flesh roughly and put in a food processor or blender.

3 Heat the olive oil in a large saucepan and gently fry the onion for 5 minutes. Stir in the garlic and chilli and cook for a further 5 minutes, stirring. Add to the food processor and blend until fairly smooth.

4 Return the mixture to the saucepan with the tomatoes and stir in the lemon rind and juice. Season to taste with salt and pepper. Add 2–3 tablespoons of vegetable stock if the sauce is a little thick. Bring to the boil and bubble for 1–2 minutes.

5 Meanwhile, bring a large saucepan of lightly salted water to the boil and cook the pasta for 10 minutes, or until 'al dente'. Drain thoroughly. Add the sauce and toss well to coat.

6 Tip into a warmed serving dish or on to individual plates. Scatter with shavings of Parmesan cheese and a few basil leaves before serving.

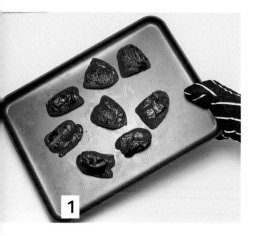

1

3

5

Rigatoni with Oven–dried Cherry Tomatoes & Mascarpone

INGREDIENTS

Serves 4

350 g/12 oz red cherry tomatoes
1 tsp caster sugar
salt and freshly ground black pepper
2 tbsp olive oil
400 g/14 oz dried rigatoni
125 g/4 oz petits pois
2 tbsp mascarpone cheese
1 tbsp freshly chopped mint
1 tbsp freshly chopped parsley
sprigs of fresh mint, to garnish

1 Preheat the oven to 140°C/275°F/Gas Mark 1. Halve the cherry tomatoes and place close together on a non-stick baking tray, cut-side up. Sprinkle lightly with the sugar, then with a little salt and pepper. Bake in the preheated oven for 1¼ hours, or until dry, but not beginning to colour. Leave to cool on the baking tray. Put in a bowl, drizzle over the olive oil and toss to coat.

2 Bring a large saucepan of lightly salted water to the boil and cook the pasta for about 10 minutes or until 'al dente'. Add the petits pois 2–3 minutes before the end of the cooking time. Drain thoroughly and return the pasta and the petits pois to the saucepan.

3 Add the mascarpone to the saucepan. When melted, add the tomatoes, mint, parsley and a little black pepper. Toss gently together, then transfer to a warmed serving dish or individual plates and garnish with sprigs of fresh mint. Serve immediately.

TASTY TIP

Double the quantity of tomatoes. When cooked, pack tightly into a sterilised jar layered up with fresh herbs and garlic. Cover with olive oil and leave in the refrigerator for a few days. Use as above or serve as an antipasto with bread, cold meats and olives. Do not keep for longer than two weeks.

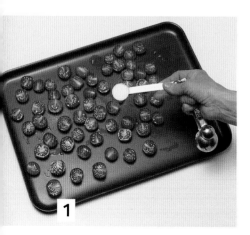

1

1

2

Spinach Dumplings with Rich Tomato Sauce

INGREDIENTS

Serves 4

For the sauce:

2 tbsp olive oil
1 onion, peeled and chopped
1 garlic clove, peeled and crushed
1 red chilli, deseeded and chopped
150 ml/¼ pint dry white wine
400 g can chopped tomatoes
pared strip of lemon rind

For the dumplings:

450 g/1 lb fresh spinach
50 g/2 oz ricotta cheese
25 g/1 oz fresh white breadcrumbs
25 g/1 oz Parmesan cheese, grated
1 medium egg yolk
¼ tsp freshly grated nutmeg
salt and freshly ground black pepper
5 tbsp plain flour
2 tbsp olive oil, for frying
fresh basil leaves, to garnish
freshly cooked tagliatelle, to serve

1 To make the tomato sauce, heat the olive oil in a large saucepan and fry the onion gently for 5 minutes. Add the garlic and chilli and cook for a further 5 minutes, until softened.

2 Stir in the wine, chopped tomatoes and lemon rind. Bring to the boil, cover and simmer for 20 minutes, then uncover and simmer for 15 minutes, or until the sauce has thickened. Remove the lemon rind and season to taste with salt and pepper.

3 To make the spinach dumplings, wash the spinach thoroughly and remove any tough stalks. Cover and cook in a large saucepan over a low heat with just the water clinging to the leaves. Drain, then squeeze out all the excess water. Finely chop and put in a large bowl.

4 Add the ricotta, breadcrumbs, Parmesan cheese and egg yolk to the spinach. Season with nutmeg and salt and pepper. Mix together and shape into 20 walnut-sized balls.

5 Toss the spinach balls in the flour. Heat the olive oil in a large non-stick frying pan and fry the balls gently for 5–6 minutes, carefully turning occasionally. Garnish with fresh basil leaves and serve immediately with the tomato sauce and tagliatelle.

2

4

5

Aubergine Cannelloni with Watercress Sauce

INGREDIENTS

Serves 4

4 large aubergines, about
 250 g/9 oz each
5–6 tbsp olive oil
350 g/12 oz ricotta cheese
75 g/3 oz Parmesan cheese, grated
3 tbsp freshly chopped basil
salt and freshly ground black pepper

For the watercress sauce:

75 g/3 oz watercress, trimmed
200 ml/⅓ pint vegetable stock
1 shallot, peeled and sliced
pared strip of lemon rind
1 large sprig of thyme
3 tbsp crème fraîche
1 tsp lemon juice

To garnish:

sprigs of watercress
lemon zest

1 Preheat the oven to 190°C/375°F/Gas Mark 5, 10 minutes before cooking. Cut the aubergines lengthways into thin slices, discarding the side pieces. Heat 2 tablespoons of oil in a frying pan and cook the aubergine slices in a single layer in several batches, turning once, until golden on both sides.

2 Mix the cheeses, basil and seasoning together. Lay the aubergine slices on a clean surface and spread the cheese mixture evenly between them.

3 Roll up the slices from one of the short ends to enclose the filling. Place, seam-side down, in a single layer in an ovenproof dish. Bake in the preheated oven for 15 minutes, or until golden.

4 To make the watercress sauce, blanch the watercress leaves in boiling water for about 30 seconds. Drain well, then rinse in a sieve under cold running water and squeeze dry. Put the stock, shallot, lemon rind and thyme in a small saucepan. Boil rapidly until reduced by half, then remove from the heat and strain.

5 Put the watercress and strained stock in a food processor and blend until fairly smooth. Return to the saucepan, stir in the crème fraîche, lemon juice and season to taste with salt and pepper. Heat gently until the sauce is piping hot.

6 Serve a little of the sauce drizzled over the aubergines and the rest separately in a jug. Garnish the cannelloni with sprigs of watercress and lemon zest. Serve immediately.

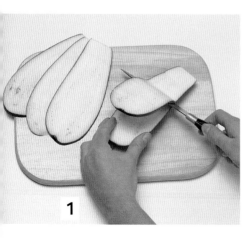
1

2

5

Panzanella

INGREDIENTS

Serves 4

250 g/9 oz day-old Italian-style bread

1 tbsp red wine vinegar

4 tbsp olive oil

1 tsp lemon juice

1 small garlic clove, peeled
  and finely chopped

1 red onion, peeled and finely sliced

1 cucumber, peeled if preferred

225 g/8 oz ripe tomatoes, deseeded

150 g/5 oz pitted black olives

about 20 basil leaves, coarsely torn or
  left whole if small

sea salt and freshly ground
  black pepper

TASTY TIP

Choose an open-textured Italian-style bread such as ciabatta for this classic Tuscany salad. Look in your local delicatessen for different flavoured marinated olives. Try chilli and garlic, or basil, garlic and orange.

1 Cut the bread into thick slices, leaving the crusts on. Add 1 teaspoon of red wine vinegar to a jug of iced water, put the slices of bread in a bowl and pour over the water. Make sure the bread is covered completely. Leave to soak for 3–4 minutes until just soft.

2 Remove the soaked bread from the water and squeeze it gently, first with your hands and then in a clean tea towel to remove any excess water. Put the bread on a plate, cover with clingfilm and chill in the refrigerator for about 1 hour.

3 Meanwhile, whisk together the olive oil, the remaining red wine vinegar and lemon juice in a large serving bowl. Add the garlic and onion and stir to coat well.

4 Halve the cucumber and remove the seeds. Chop both the cucumber and tomatoes into 1 cm/½ inch cubes. Add to the garlic and onions with the olives. Tear the bread into bite-sized chunks and add to the bowl with the fresh basil leaves. Toss together to mix and serve immediately, with a grinding of sea salt and black pepper.

2

3

4

Vegetable Frittata

INGREDIENTS

Serves 2

6 medium eggs
2 tbsp freshly chopped parsley
1 tbsp freshly chopped tarragon
25 g/1 oz pecorino or Parmesan
  cheese, finely grated
freshly ground black pepper
175 g/6 oz tiny new potatoes
2 small carrots, peeled and sliced
125 g/4 oz broccoli, cut into
  small florets
1 courgette, about 125 g/4 oz, sliced
2 tbsp olive oil
4 spring onions, trimmed and
  thinly sliced

To serve:
mixed green salad
crusty Italian bread

FOOD FACT

A frittata is a heavy omelette, usually with a vegetable, meat or cheese filling that is cooked slowly and often finished in the oven or under the grill. It is closer to a Spanish tortilla than to a classic French omelette.

1 Preheat grill just before cooking. Lightly beat the eggs with the parsley, tarragon and half the cheese. Season to taste with black pepper and reserve. (Salt is not needed as the pecorino is very salty.)

2 Bring a large saucepan of lightly salted water to the boil. Add the new potatoes and cook for 8 minutes. Add the carrots and cook for 4 minutes, then add the broccoli florets and the courgettes and cook for a further 3–4 minutes, or until all the vegetables are barely tender. Drain well.

3 Heat the oil in a 20.5 cm/8 inch heavy-based frying pan. Add the spring onions and cook for 3–4 minutes, or until softened. Add all the vegetables and cook for a few seconds, then pour in the beaten egg mixture.

4 Stir gently for about a minute, then cook for a further 1–2 minutes, or until the bottom of the frittata is set and golden brown.

5 Place the pan under a hot grill for 1 minute, or until almost set and just beginning to brown. Sprinkle with the remaining cheese and grill for a further 1 minute, or until it is lightly browned.

6 Loosen the edges and slide out of the pan. Cut into wedges and serve hot or warm with a mixed green salad and crusty Italian bread.

2

3

5

Panzerotti

INGREDIENTS

Serves 16

450 g/1 lb strong white flour
pinch of salt
1 tsp easy-blend dried yeast
2 tbsp olive oil
300 ml/½ pint warm water
fresh rocket leaves, to serve

For the filling:

1 tbsp olive oil
1 small red onion, peeled and
  finely chopped
2 garlic cloves, peeled and crushed
½ yellow pepper, deseeded
  and chopped
1 small courgette, about 75 g/
  3 oz, trimmed and chopped
50 g/2 oz black olives,
  pitted and quartered
125 g/4 oz mozzarella cheese,
  cut into tiny cubes
salt and freshly ground black pepper
5–6 tbsp tomato purée
1 tsp dried mixed herbs
oil for deep-frying

1   Sift the flour and salt into a bowl. Stir in the yeast. Make a well in the centre. Add the oil and the warm water and mix to a soft dough. Knead on a lightly floured surface until smooth and elastic. Put in an oiled bowl, cover and leave in a warm place to rise while making the filling.

2   To make the filling, heat the oil in a frying pan and cook the onion for 5 minutes. Add the garlic, yellow pepper and courgette. Cook for about 5 minutes, or until the vegetables are tender. Tip into a bowl and leave to cool slightly. Stir in the olives, mozzarella cheese and season to taste with salt and pepper.

3   Briefly reknead the dough. Divide into 16 equal pieces. Roll out each to a circle about 10 cm/4 inches across. Mix together the tomato purée and dried herbs, then spread about 1 teaspoon on each circle, leaving a 2 cm/¾ inch border around the edge.

4   Divide the filling equally between the circles – it will seem a small amount, but if you overfill, they will leak during cooking. Brush the edges with water, then fold in half to enclose the filling. Press to seal, then crimp the edges.

5   Heat the oil in a deep-fat fryer to 180°C/350°F. Deep-fry the panzerotti in batches for 3 minutes, or until golden. Drain on absorbent kitchen paper and keep warm in a low oven until ready to serve with fresh rocket.

Pasta Primavera

INGREDIENTS

Serves 4

150 g/5 oz French beans
150 g/5 oz sugar snap peas
40 g/1½ oz butter
1 tsp olive oil
225 g/8 oz baby carrots, scrubbed
2 courgettes, trimmed and
  thinly sliced
175 g/6 oz baby leeks, trimmed and
  cut into 2.5 cm/1 inch lengths
200 ml/7 fl oz double cream
1 tsp finely grated lemon rind
350 g/12 oz dried tagliatelle
25 g/1 oz Parmesan cheese, grated
1 tbsp freshly snipped chives
1 tbsp freshly chopped dill
salt and freshly ground black pepper
sprigs of fresh dill, to garnish

FOOD FACT

Primavera means 'spring' and this dish is classically made with spring vegetables. At other times, use available baby vegetables.

1 Trim and halve the French beans. Bring a large saucepan of lightly salted water to the boil and cook the beans for 4–5 minutes, adding the sugar snap peas after 2 minutes, so that both are tender at the same time. Drain the beans and sugar snap peas and briefly rinse under cold running water.

2 Heat the butter and oil in a large non-stick frying pan. Add the baby carrots and cook for 2 minutes, then stir in the courgettes and leeks and cook for 10 minutes, stirring, until the vegetables are almost tender.

3 Stir the cream and lemon rind into the vegetables and bubble over a gentle heat until the sauce is slightly reduced and the vegetables are cooked.

4 Meanwhile, bring a large saucepan of lightly salted water to the boil and cook the tagliatelle for 10 minutes, or until 'al dente'.

5 Add the beans, sugar snaps, Parmesan cheese and herbs to the sauce. Stir for 30 seconds, or until the cheese has melted and the vegetables are hot.

6 Drain the tagliatelle, add the vegetables and sauce, then toss gently to mix and season to taste with salt and pepper. Spoon into a warmed serving bowl and garnish with a few sprigs of dill and serve immediately.

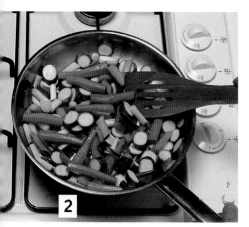

Spaghetti with Pesto

INGREDIENTS

Serves 4

200 g/7 oz freshly grated Parmesan
  cheese, plus extra to serve
25 g/1 oz fresh basil leaves, plus extra
  to garnish
6 tbsp pine nuts
3 large garlic cloves, peeled
200 ml/7 fl oz extra virgin olive oil,
  plus more if necessary
salt and freshly ground pepper
400 g/14 oz spaghetti

HELPFUL HINT

You can still make pesto if you do
not have a food processor. Tear
the basil leaves and place them
in a mortar with the garlic, pine
nuts and a tablespoonful of the
oil. Pound to a paste using a
pestle, gradually working in the
rest of the oil. Transfer to a bowl
and stir in the cheese. Season to
taste with salt and pepper. Pesto
will keep for 2–3 days if stored in
the refrigerator.

1 To make the pesto, place the Parmesan cheese in a food
processor with the basil leaves, pine nuts and garlic and process
until well blended.

2 With the motor running, gradually pour in the extra virgin olive oil,
until a thick sauce forms. Add a little more oil if the sauce seems
too thick. Season to taste with salt and pepper. Transfer to a bowl,
cover and store in the refrigerator until required.

3 Bring a large pan of lightly salted water to a rolling boil. Add the
spaghetti and cook according to the packet instructions, or until
'al dente'.

4 Drain the spaghetti thoroughly and return to the pan. Stir in the
pesto and toss lightly. Heat through gently, then tip the pasta into a
warmed serving dish or spoon on to individual plates. Garnish with
basil leaves and serve immediately with extra Parmesan cheese.

1

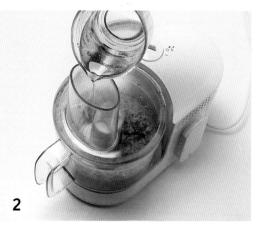

2

4

Pasta Shells with Broccoli & Capers

INGREDIENTS

Serves 4

400 g/14 oz conchiglie (shells)
450 g/1 lb broccoli florets, cut into
  small pieces
5 tbsp olive oil
1 large onion, peeled and
  finely chopped
4 tbsp capers in brine, rinsed
  and drained
½ tsp dried chilli flakes (optional)
75 g/3 oz freshly grated Parmesan
  cheese, plus extra to serve
25 g/1 oz pecorino cheese, grated
salt and freshly ground black pepper
2 tbsp freshly chopped flat leaf
  parsley, to garnish

HELPFUL HINT

Chilli flakes are made from dried, crushed chillies and add a pungent hot spiciness to this dish. There are lots of other chilli products that you could use instead. For instance, substitute a tablespoonful of chilli oil for one of the tablespoons of olive oil or add a dash of tabasco sauce at the end of cooking.

1 Bring a large pan of lightly salted water to a rolling boil. Add the pasta shells, return to the boil and cook for 2 minutes. Add the broccoli to the pan. Return to the boil and continue cooking for 8–10 minutes, or until the conchiglie is 'al dente'.

2 Meanwhile, heat the olive oil in a large frying pan, add the onion and cook for 5 minutes, or until softened, stirring frequently. Stir in the capers and chilli flakes, if using, and cook for a further 2 minutes.

3 Drain the pasta and broccoli and add to the frying pan. Toss the ingredients to mix thoroughly. Sprinkle over the cheeses, then stir until the cheeses have just melted. Season to taste with salt and pepper, then tip into a warmed serving dish. Garnish with chopped parsley and serve immediately with extra Parmesan cheese.

Venetian Herb Orzo

INGREDIENTS

Serves 4-6

200 g/7 oz baby spinach leaves
150 g/5 oz rocket leaves
50 g/2 oz flat leaf parsley
6 spring onions, trimmed
few leaves of fresh mint
3 tbsp extra virgin olive oil, plus
   more if required
450 g/11 oz orzo
salt and freshly ground black pepper

FOOD FACT

Rocket was first introduced to Britain in the late sixteenth century, but went out of fashion during Victorian times. It adds a peppery flavour to many dishes. The tender tiny leaves have the most delicate flavour and as they grow in size, the flavour becomes more pronounced.

1 Rinse the spinach leaves in several changes of cold water and reserve. Finely chop the rocket leaves with the parsley and mint. Thinly slice the green of the spring onions.

2 Bring a large saucepan of water to the boil, add the spinach leaves, herbs and spring onions and cook for about 10 seconds. Remove and rinse under cold running water. Drain well and, using your hands, squeeze out all the excess moisture.

3 Place the spinach, herbs and spring onions in a food processor. Blend for 1 minute then, with the motor running, gradually pour in the olive oil until the sauce is well blended.

4 Meanwhile, bring a large pan of lightly salted water to a rolling boil. Add the pasta and cook according to the packet instructions, or until 'al dente'. Drain thoroughly and place in a large warmed bowl.

5 Add the spinach sauce to the orzo and stir lightly until the orzo is well coated. Stir in an extra tablespoon of olive oil if the mixture seems too thick. Season well with salt and pepper. Serve immediately on warmed plates or allow to cool to room temperature.

1

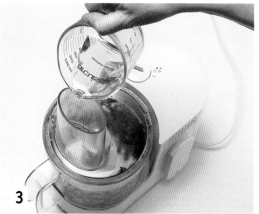

3

5

Cheesy Pasta with Tomatoes & Cream

INGREDIENTS

Serves 4

shop-bought fresh pasta dough
225 g/8 oz fresh ricotta cheese
225 g/8 oz smoked mozzarella,
  grated, (use normal if smoked
  is unavailable)
5 g/4 oz freshly grated pecorino or
  Parmesan cheese
2 medium eggs, lightly beaten
2–3 tbsp finely chopped mint,
  basil or parsley
salt and freshly ground black pepper

For the sauce:

2 tbsp olive oil
1 small onion, peeled and
  finely chopped
2 garlic cloves, peeled and
  finely chopped
450g/1 lb ripe plum tomatoes,
  peeled, deseeded and
  finely chopped
50 ml/2 fl oz white vermouth
225 ml/8 fl oz double cream
fresh basil leaves, to garnish

1 Place the ricotta cheese in a bowl and beat until smooth, then add the remaining cheeses with the eggs, herbs and seasoning to taste. Beat well until creamy and smooth.

2 Cut the prepared pasta dough into quarters. Working with one quarter at a time, and covering the remaining quarters with a clean, damp tea towel, roll out the pasta very thinly. Using a 10 cm/4 inch pastry cutter or small saucer, cut out as many rounds as possible.

3 Place a small tablespoonful of the filling mixture slightly below the centre of each round. Lightly moisten the edge of the round with water and fold in half to form a filled half-moon shape. Using a dinner fork, press the edges together firmly.

4 Transfer to a lightly floured baking sheet and continue filling the remaining pasta. Leave to dry for 15 minutes.

5 Heat the oil in a large saucepan, add the onions and cook for 3–4 minutes, or until beginning to soften. Add the garlic and cook for 1–2 minutes, then add the tomatoes, vermouth and cream and bring to the boil. Simmer for 10–15 minutes, or until thickened and reduced.

6 Bring a large saucepan of salted water to the boil. Add the filled pasta and return to the boil. Cook, stirring frequently to prevent sticking, for 5 minutes, or until 'al dente'. Drain and return to the pan. Pour over the tomato and cream sauce, garnish with basil leaves and serve immediately.

1

2

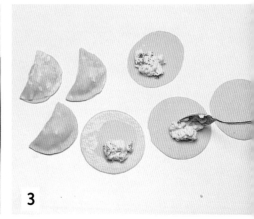

3

Pastini-stuffed Peppers

INGREDIENTS

Serves 6

6 red, yellow or orange peppers,
  tops cut off and deseeded
salt and freshly ground black pepper
175 g/6 oz pastini
4 tbsp olive oil
1 onion, peeled and finely chopped
2 garlic cloves, peeled and
  finely chopped
3 ripe plum tomatoes, skinned,
  deseeded and chopped
50 ml/2 fl oz dry white wine
8 pitted black olives, chopped
4 tbsp freshly chopped mixed
  herbs, such as parsley, basil,
  oregano or marjoram
125 g/4 oz mozzarella cheese, diced
4 tbsp grated Parmesan cheese
fresh tomato sauce, preferably
  home-made, to serve

1 Preheat the oven to 190°C/375°F/Gas Mark 5, 10 minutes before cooking. Bring a pan of water to the boil. Trim the bottom of each pepper so it sits straight. Blanch the peppers for 2–3 minutes, then drain on absorbent kitchen paper.

2 Return the water to the boil, add ½ teaspoon of salt and the pastini and cook for 3–4 minutes, or until 'al dente'. Drain thoroughly, reserving the water. Rinse under cold running water, drain again and reserve.

3 Heat 2 tablespoons of the olive oil in a large frying pan, add the onion and cook for 3–4 minutes. Add the garlic and cook for 1 minute. Stir in the tomatoes and wine and cook for 5 minutes, stirring frequently. Add the olives, herbs, mozzarella cheese and half the Parmesan cheese. Season to taste with salt and pepper. Remove from the heat and stir in the pastini.

4 Dry the insides of the peppers with absorbent kitchen paper, then season lightly. Arrange the peppers in a lightly oiled shallow baking dish and fill with the pastini mixture. Sprinkle with the remaining Parmesan cheese and drizzle over the remaining oil. Pour in boiling water to come 1 cm/½ inch up the sides of the dish. Cook in the preheated oven for 25 minutes, or until cooked. Serve immediately with freshly made tomato sauce.

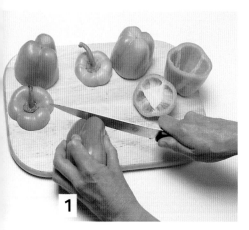

1

3

4

Fusilli with Courgettes & Sun-dried Tomatoes

INGREDIENTS

Serves 6

5 tbsp olive oil

1 large onion, peeled and thinly sliced

2 garlic cloves, peeled and
  finely chopped

700 g/1½ lb courgettes, trimmed
  and sliced

400 g can chopped plum tomatoes

12 sun-dried tomatoes, cut into
  thin strips

salt and freshly ground black pepper

450 g/1 lb fusilli

25 g/1 oz butter, diced

2 tbsp freshly chopped basil or
  flat leaf parsley

grated Parmesan or pecorino
  cheese, for serving

FOOD FACT

Sun-dried tomatoes come in jars with olive oil or simply dried in packets. The latter are better here as they will soak up the juices from the chopped tomatoes and courgettes and help to thicken the sauce.

1 Heat 2 tablespoons of the olive oil in a large frying pan, add the onion and cook for 5–7 minutes, or until softened. Add the chopped garlic and courgette slices and cook for a further 5 minutes, stirring occasionally.

2 Stir the chopped tomatoes and the sun-dried tomatoes into the frying pan and season to taste with salt and pepper. Cook until the courgettes are just tender and the sauce is slightly thickened.

3 Bring a large pan of lightly salted water to a rolling boil. Add the fusilli and cook according to the packet instructions, or until 'al dente'.

4 Drain the fusilli thoroughly and return to the pan. Add the butter and remaining oil and toss to coat. Stir the chopped basil or parsley into the courgette mixture and pour over the fusilli. Toss and tip into a warmed serving dish. Serve with grated Parmesan or pecorino cheese.

1

2

4

Linguine with Walnut Pesto

INGREDIENTS

Serves 4

125 g/4 oz walnut halves
1–2 garlic cloves, peeled and
   coarsely chopped
40 g/1½ oz dried breadcrumbs
3 tbsp extra virgin olive oil
1 tbsp walnut oil
3–4 tbsp freshly chopped parsley
50 g/2 oz butter, softened
2 tbsp double cream
25 g/1 oz Parmesan cheese, grated,
   plus extra to serve
salt and freshly ground black pepper
450 g/1 lb linguine

HELPFUL HINT

It is important to use dried breadcrumbs for this recipe. Avoid the bright orange variety, which are unsuitable. Spread about 50 g/2 oz fresh breadcrumbs (they will weigh less when dried) on a baking sheet and bake in a very low oven for about 20–25 minutes, stirring occasionally, until dry but not coloured.

1 Bring a saucepan of water to the boil. Add the walnut halves and simmer for about 1 minute. Drain and turn on to a clean tea towel. Using the towel, rub the nuts gently to loosen the skins, turn into a coarse sieve or colander and shake to separate. Discard the skins and coarsely chop the nuts.

2 With the the food processor motor running, drop in the garlic cloves and chop finely. Remove the lid, then add the walnuts, breadcrumbs, olive and walnut oils and the parsley. Blend to a paste with a crumbly texture.

3 Scrape the nut mixture into a bowl, add the softened butter and, using a wooden spoon, cream them together. Gradually beat in the cream and the Parmesan cheese. Season the walnut pesto to taste with salt and pepper.

4 Bring a large pan of lightly salted water to a rolling boil. Add the linguine and cook according to the packet instructions, or until 'al dente'.

5 Drain the linguine thoroughly, reserving 1–2 tablespoons of the cooking water. Return the linguine and reserved water to the pan. Add the walnut pesto, 1 tablespoon at a time, tossing and stirring until well coated. Tip into a warmed serving dish or spoon on to individual plates. Serve immediately with the extra grated Parmesan cheese.

1

2

3

Four-cheese Tagliatelle

INGREDIENTS

Serves 4

300 ml/½ pint whipping cream
4 garlic cloves, peeled and
  lightly bruised
75 g/3 oz fontina cheese, diced
75 g/3 oz Gruyère cheese, grated
75 g/3 oz mozzarella cheese, cubed
50 g/2 oz Parmesan cheese, grated,
  plus extra to serve
salt and freshly ground black pepper
275 g/10 oz fresh green tagliatelle
1–2 tbsp freshly snipped chives
fresh basil leaves, to garnish

HELPFUL HINT

Fresh pasta takes much less time to cook than dried pasta and 2–3 minutes is usually long enough for it to be 'al dente', but check the packet for cooking instructions. Green tagliatelle is generally flavoured with spinach, but it is also available flavoured with fresh herbs, which would go particularly well with the rich cheese sauce in this recipe.

1 Place the whipping cream with the garlic cloves in a medium pan and heat gently until small bubbles begin to form around the edge of the pan. Using a slotted spoon, remove and discard the garlic cloves.

2 Add all the cheeses to the pan and stir until melted. Season with a little salt and a lot of black pepper. Keep the sauce warm over a low heat, but do not allow to boil.

3 Meanwhile, bring a large pan of lightly salted water to the boil. Add the tagliatelle, return to the boil and cook for 2–3 minutes, or until 'al dente'.

4 Drain the pasta thoroughly and return to the pan. Pour the sauce over the pasta, add the chives then toss lightly until well coated. Tip into a warmed serving dish or spoon on to individual plates. Garnish with a few basil leaves and serve immediately with extra Parmesan cheese.

Spaghetti alla Puttanesca

INGREDIENTS

Serves 4

4 tbsp olive oil

2 garlic cloves, peeled and
  finely chopped

½ tsp crushed dried chillies

400 g can chopped plum tomatoes

125 g/4 oz pitted black olives,
  cut in half

2 tbsp capers, rinsed and drained

1 tsp freshly chopped oregano

1 tbsp tomato paste

salt and freshly ground black pepper

400 g/14 oz spaghetti

2 tbsp freshly chopped parsley

1 Heat the olive oil in a large frying pan, add the garlic and dried chillies and cook for 1 minute, stirring frequently.

2 Add the tomatoes, olives, capers, oregano and tomato paste and cook, stirring occasionally, for 15 minutes, or until the liquid has evaporated and the sauce is thickened. Season the tomato sauce to taste with salt and pepper.

3 Meanwhile, bring a large pan of lightly salted water to a rolling boil. Add the spaghetti and cook according to the packet instructions, or until 'al dente'.

4 Drain the spaghetti thoroughly, reserving 1–2 tablespoons of the the cooking water. Return the spaghetti with the reserved water to the pan. Pour the tomato sauce over the spaghetti, add the chopped parsley and toss to coat. Tip into a warmed serving dish or spoon on to individual plates and serve immediately.

Tagliatelle Primavera

INGREDIENTS

Serves 4

125 g/4 oz asparagus, lightly peeled and
cut into 6.5 cm/2½ inch lengths

125 g/4 oz carrots, peeled and cut
into julienne strips

125 g/4 oz courgettes, trimmed and
cut into julienne strips

50 g/2 oz small mangetout

50 g/2 oz butter

1 small onion, peeled and
finely chopped

1 small red pepper, deseeded
and finely chopped

50 ml/2 fl oz dry vermouth

225 ml/8 fl oz double cream

1 small leek, trimmed and cut
into julienne strips

75 g/3 oz fresh green peas
(or frozen, thawed)

salt and freshly ground black pepper

400 g/14 oz fresh tagliatelle

2 tbsp freshly chopped flat leaf parsley

25 g/1 oz Parmesan cheese, grated

1 Bring a medium saucepan of salted water to the boil. Add the asparagus and blanch for 1–2 minutes, or until just beginning to soften. Using a slotted spoon, transfer to a colander and rinse under cold running water. Repeat with the carrots and courgettes. Add the mangetout, return to the boil, drain, rinse immediately and drain again. Reserve the blanched vegetables.

2 Heat the butter in a large frying pan, add the onion and red pepper and cook for 5 minutes, or until they begin to soften and colour. Pour in the dry vermouth; it will bubble and steam and evaporate almost immediately. Stir in the cream and simmer over a medium-low heat until reduced by about half. Add the blanched vegetables with the leeks, peas and seasoning and heat through for 2 minutes.

3 Meanwhile, bring a large saucepan of lightly salted water to the boil, add the tagliatelle and return to the boil. Cook for 2–3 minutes, or until 'al dente'. Drain thoroughly and return to the pan.

4 Stir the chopped parsley into the cream and vegetable sauce then pour over the pasta and toss to coat. Sprinkle with the grated Parmesan cheese and toss lightly. Tip into a warmed serving bowl or spoon on to individual plates and serve immediately.

Aubergine & Ravioli Parmigiana

INGREDIENTS

Serves 6

4 tbsp olive oil

1 large onion, peeled and
finely chopped

2–3 garlic cloves, peeled and crushed

2 x 400 g cans chopped tomatoes

2 tsp brown sugar

1 dried bay leaf

1 tsp dried oregano

1 tsp dried basil

2 tbsp freshly shredded basil

salt and freshly ground black pepper

2–3 medium aubergines, sliced
cross-wise 1 cm/½ inch thick

2 medium eggs, beaten with
1 tbsp water

125 g/4 oz dried breadcrumbs

75 g/3 oz freshly grated
Parmesan cheese

400 g/14 oz mozzarella cheese,
thinly sliced

250 g/9 oz cheese-filled ravioli,
cooked and drained

1 Preheat the oven to 180°C/350°F/Gas Mark 4, about 15 minutes before cooking. Heat 2 tablespoons of the olive oil in a large, heavy-based pan, add the onion and cook for 6–7 minutes, or until softened. Add the garlic, cook for 1 minute then stir in the tomatoes, sugar, bay leaf, dried oregano and basil, then bring to the boil, stirring frequently. Simmer for 30–35 minutes, or until thickened and reduced, stirring occasionally. Stir in the fresh basil and season to taste with salt and pepper. Remove the tomato sauce from the heat and reserve.

2 Heat the remaining olive oil in a large, heavy-based frying pan over a high heat. Dip the aubergine slices in the egg mixture then in the breadcrumbs. Cook in batches until golden on both sides. Drain on absorbent kitchen paper. Add more oil between batches if necessary.

3 Spoon a little tomato sauce into the base of a lightly oiled large baking dish. Cover with a layer of aubergine slices, a sprinkling of Parmesan cheese, a layer of mozzarella cheese, then more sauce. Repeat the layers then cover the sauce with a layer of cooked ravioli. Continue to layer in this way, ending with a layer of mozzarella cheese. Sprinkle the top with Parmesan cheese.

4 Drizzle with a little extra olive oil if liked, then bake in the preheated oven for 30 minutes, or until golden-brown and bubbling. Serve immediately.

Courgette Lasagne

INGREDIENTS

Serves 8

2 tbsp olive oil

1 medium onion, peeled and
   finely chopped

225 g/8 oz mushrooms, wiped
   and thinly sliced

3–4 courgettes, trimmed and
   thinly sliced

2 garlic cloves, peeled and
   finely chopped

$\frac{1}{2}$ tsp dried thyme

1–2 tbsp freshly chopped basil or
   flat leaf parsley

salt and freshly ground black pepper

1 quantity prepared white sauce

350 g/12 oz lasagne sheets, cooked

225 g/8 oz mozzarella cheese, grated

50 g/2 oz Parmesan cheese, grated

400 g can chopped tomatoes, drained

1 Preheat the oven to 200°C/400°F/Gas Mark 6, 15 minutes before cooking. Heat the oil in a large frying pan, add the onion and cook for 3–5 minutes. Add the mushrooms, cook for 2 minutes then add the courgettes and cook for a further 3–4 minutes, or until tender. Stir in the garlic, thyme and basil or parsley and season to taste with salt and pepper. Remove from the heat and reserve.

2 Spoon one-third of the white sauce on to the base of a lightly oiled large baking dish. Arrange a layer of lasagne over the sauce. Spread half the courgette mixture over the pasta, then sprinkle with some of the mozzarella and some of the Parmesan cheese. Repeat with more white sauce and another layer of lasagne, then cover with half the drained tomatoes.

3 Cover the tomatoes with lasagne, the remaining courgette mixture, and some mozzarella and Parmesan cheese. Repeat the layers ending with a layer of lasagne sheets, white sauce and the remaining Parmesan cheese. Bake in the preheated oven for 35 minutes, or until golden. Serve immediately.

1

2

3

Rigatoni with Gorgonzola & Walnuts

INGREDIENTS

Serves 4

400 g/14 oz rigatoni
50 g/2 oz butter
125 g/4 oz crumbled
  Gorgonzola cheese
2 tbsp brandy, optional
200 ml/7 fl oz whipping
  or double cream
75 g/3 oz walnut pieces, lightly
  toasted and coarsely chopped
1 tbsp freshly chopped basil
50 g/2 oz freshly grated
  Parmesan cheese
salt and freshly ground black pepper

To serve:

cherry tomatoes
fresh green salad leaves

1 Bring a large pan of lightly salted water to a rolling boil. Add the rigatoni and cook according to the packet instructions, or until 'al dente'. Drain the pasta thoroughly, reserve and keep warm.

2 Melt the butter in a large saucepan or wok over a medium heat. Add the Gorgonzola cheese and stir until just melted. Add the brandy if using and cook for 30 seconds, then pour in the cream and cook for 1–2 minutes, stirring until the sauce is smooth.

3 Stir in the walnut pieces, basil and half the Parmesan cheese, then add the rigatoni. Season to taste with salt and pepper. Return to the heat, stirring frequently, until heated through. Divide the pasta among four warmed pasta bowls, sprinkle with the remaining Parmesan cheese and serve immediately with cherry tomatoes and fresh green salad leaves.

Pumpkin–filled Pasta with Butter & Sage

INGREDIENTS

Serves 6-8

1 quantity bought fresh pasta dough
125 g/4 oz butter
2 tbsp freshly shredded sage leaves
50 g/2 oz freshly grated Parmesan
   cheese, to serve

For the filling:

250 g/9 oz freshly cooked
   pumpkin or sweet potato flesh,
   mashed and cooled
75–125 g/3–4 oz dried breadcrumbs
125 g/4 oz freshly grated
   Parmesan cheese
1 medium egg yolk
1/2 tsp soft brown sugar
2 tbsp freshly chopped parsley
freshly grated nutmeg
salt and freshly ground black pepper

1 Mix together the ingredients for the filling in a bowl, seasoning to taste with freshly grated nutmeg, salt and pepper. If the mixture seems too wet, add a few more breadcrumbs to bind.

2 Cut the pasta dough into quarters. Work with one quarter at a time, covering the remaining quarters with a damp tea towel. Roll out a quarter very thinly into a strip 10 cm/4 inches wide. Drop spoonfuls of the filling along the strip 6.5 cm/2½ inches apart, in two rows about 5 cm/2 inches apart. Moisten the outside edges and the spaces between the filling with water.

3 Roll out another strip of pasta and lay it over the filled strip. Press down gently along both edges and between the filled sections. Using a fluted pastry wheel, cut along both long sides, down the centre and between the fillings to form cushions. Transfer the cushions to a lightly floured baking sheet. Continue making cushions and allow to dry for 30 minutes.

4 Bring a large saucepan of slightly salted water to the boil. Add the pasta cushions and return to the boil. Cook, stirring frequently, for 4–5 minutes, or until 'al dente'. Drain carefully.

5 Heat the butter in a pan, stir in the shredded sage leaves and cook for 30 seconds. Add the pasta cushions, stir gently then spoon into serving bowls. Sprinkle with the grated Parmesan cheese and serve immediately.

1

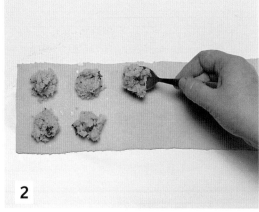

2

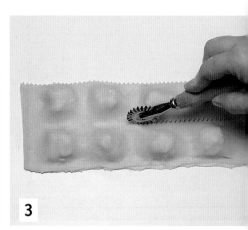

3

Tortellini, Cherry Tomato & Mozzarella Skewers

INGREDIENTS

Serves 6

250 g/9 oz mixed green and
   plain cheese or vegetable-filled
   fresh tortellini
150 ml/¼ pint extra virgin olive oil
2 garlic cloves, peeled and crushed
pinch dried thyme or basil
salt and freshly ground black pepper
225 g/8 oz cherry tomatoes
450 g/1 lb mozzarella, cut into
   2.5 cm/1 inch cubes
basil leaves, to garnish
dressed salad leaves, to serve

HELPFUL HINT

These skewers make an ideal starter for a barbecue. Alternatively, a small quantity of the prepared ingredients can be threaded on to smaller skewers and served as canapés. If using wooden skewers for this recipe, soak them in cold water for at least 30 minutes before cooking to prevent them scorching under the grill.

1 Preheat the grill and line a grill pan with tinfoil, just before cooking. Bring a large pan of lightly salted water to a rolling boil. Add the tortellini and cook according to the packet instructions, or until 'al dente'. Drain, rinse under cold running water, drain again and toss with 2 tablespoons of the olive oil and reserve.

2 Pour the remaining olive oil into a small bowl. Add the crushed garlic and thyme or basil, then blend well. Season to taste with salt and black pepper and reserve.

3 To assemble the skewers, thread the tortellini alternately with the cherry tomatoes and cubes of mozzarella. Arrange the skewers on the grill pan and brush generously on all sides with the olive oil mixture.

4 Cook the skewers under the preheated grill for about 5 minutes, or until they begin to turn golden, turning them halfway through cooking. Arrange two skewers on each plate and garnish with a few basil leaves. Serve immediately with dressed salad leaves.

2

3

4

Gnocchi Roulade with Mozzarella & Spinach

INGREDIENTS

Serves 8

600 ml/1 pint milk
125 g/4 oz fine semolina or polenta
25 g/1 oz butter
75 g/3 oz Cheddar cheese, grated
2 medium egg yolks
salt and freshly ground black pepper
700 g/1½ lb baby spinach leaves
½ tsp freshly grated nutmeg
1 garlic clove, peeled and crushed
2 tbsp olive oil
150 g/5 oz mozzarella cheese, grated
2 tbsp freshly grated Parmesan cheese
freshly made tomato sauce, to serve

HELPFUL HINT

It is important to use the correct size of tin for this dish, so that the gnocchi mixture is thin enough to roll up. Do not be tempted to put it in the refrigerator to cool or it will become too hard and crack when rolled.

1 Preheat the oven to 240°C/475°F/Gas Mark 9, 15 minutes before cooking. Oil and line a large Swiss roll tin 23 x 33 cm/9 x 13 inch) with non-stick baking parchment.

2 Pour the milk into a heavy-based pan and whisk in the semolina. Bring to the boil then simmer, stirring continuously with a wooden spoon, for 3–4 minutes, or until very thick. Remove from the heat and stir in the butter and Cheddar cheese until melted. Whisk in the egg yolks and season to taste with salt and pepper. Pour into the lined tin. Cover and allow to cool for 1 hour.

3 Cook the baby spinach in batches in a large pan with 1 teaspoon of water for 3–4 minutes, or until wilted. Drain thoroughly, season to taste with salt, pepper and nutmeg, then allow to cool.

4 Spread the spinach over the cooled semolina mixture and sprinkle over 75 g/3 oz of the mozzarella and half the Parmesan cheese. Bake in the preheated oven for 20 minutes, or until golden.

5 Allow to cool, then roll up like a Swiss roll. Sprinkle with the remaining mozzarella and Parmesan cheese, then bake for another 15–20 minutes, or until golden. Serve immediately with freshly made tomato sauce.

2

4

5

Cannelloni with Tomato & Red Wine Sauce

INGREDIENTS

Serves 6

2 tbsp olive oil

1 onion, peeled and finely chopped

1 garlic clove, peeled and crushed

250 g carton ricotta cheese

50 g/2 oz pine nuts

salt and freshly ground black pepper

pinch freshly grated nutmeg

250 g/9 oz fresh spinach lasagne

25 g/1 oz butter

1 shallot, peeled and finely chopped

150 ml/¼ pint red wine

400 g can chopped tomatoes

½ tsp sugar

50 g/2 oz mozzarella cheese, grated,
   plus extra to serve

1 tbsp freshly chopped parsley,
   to garnish

fresh green salad, to serve

FOOD FACT

Mozzarella is the Italian cheese used to top pizzas, as it is elastic and stringy when cooked. It is a soft, kneaded cheese with a delicate texture. Traditionally, it was made from buffalo milk, but cows' milk is more common.

1 Preheat the oven to 200°C/400°F/Gas Mark 6, 15 minutes before cooking. Heat the oil in a heavy-based pan, add the onion and garlic and cook for 2–3 minutes. Cool slightly, then stir in the ricotta cheese and pine nuts. Season the filling to taste with salt, pepper and the nutmeg.

2 Cut each lasagne sheet in half, put a little of the ricotta filling on each piece and roll up like a cigar to resemble cannelloni tubes. Arrange the cannelloni, seam-side down in a single layer, in a lightly oiled, 2.3 litre/4 pint shallow ovenproof dish.

3 Melt the butter in a pan, add the shallot and cook for 2 minutes. Pour in the red wine, tomatoes and sugar and season well. Bring to the boil, lower the heat and simmer for about 20 minutes, or until thickened. Add a little more sugar if desired. Transfer to a food processor and blend until a smooth sauce is formed.

4 Pour the warm tomato sauce over the cannelloni and sprinkle with the grated mozzarella cheese. Bake in the preheated oven for about 30 minutes, or until golden and bubbling. Garnish and serve immediately with a green salad.

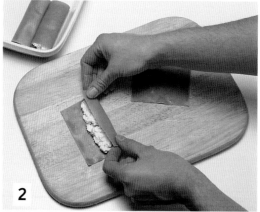

Aubergine & Tomato Layer

INGREDIENTS

Serves 4

2 aubergines, about 700 g/1½ lb,
  trimmed and thinly sliced
6 tbsp olive oil
1 onion, peeled and finely sliced
1 garlic clove, peeled and crushed
400 g can chopped tomatoes
50 ml/2 fl oz red wine
½ tsp sugar
salt and freshly ground black pepper
50 g/2 oz butter
40 g/1½ oz flour
450 ml/¾ pint milk
225 g/8 oz fresh egg lasagne
2 medium eggs, beaten
200 ml/7 fl oz Greek yogurt
125 g/3 oz mozzarella cheese, grated
fresh basil leaves, to garnish

FOOD FACT

Greek yogurt can be made from either ewes' or cows' milk. Ewes' milk is very rich and creamy, with a fat content of around 6 per cent. Cows' milk has less fat, so the yogurt is strained to concentrate it.

1 Preheat the oven to 190°C/375°F/Gas Mark 5, 10 minutes before cooking. Brush the aubergine slices with 5 tablespoons of the olive oil and place on a baking sheet. Bake in the preheated oven for 20 minutes, or until tender. Remove from the oven and increase the temperature to 200°C/400°F/Gas Mark 6.

2 Heat the remaining oil in a heavy-based pan. Add the onion and garlic, cook for 2–3 minutes then add the tomatoes, wine and sugar. Season to taste with salt and pepper, then simmer for 20 minutes.

3 Melt the butter in another pan. Stir in the flour, cook for 2 minutes, then whisk in the milk. Cook for 2–3 minutes, or until thickened. Season to taste.

4 Pour a little white sauce into a lightly oiled, 1.7 litre/3 pint baking dish. Cover with a layer of lasagne, spread with tomato sauce, then add some of the aubergines. Cover thinly with white sauce and sprinkle with a little cheese. Continue to layer in this way, finishing with a layer of lasagne.

5 Beat together the eggs and yogurt. Season, then pour over the lasagne. Sprinkle with the remaining cheese and bake in the preheated oven for 25–30 minutes, or until golden. Garnish with basil leaves and serve.

1

2

4

Ratatouille & Pasta Bake

INGREDIENTS

Serves 4

1 tbsp olive oil

2 large onions, peeled and
  finely chopped

400 g can chopped tomatoes

100 ml/3½ fl oz white wine

½ tsp caster sugar

salt and freshly ground black pepper

40 g/1½ oz butter

2 garlic cloves, peeled and crushed

125 g/4 oz mushrooms, wiped and
  thickly sliced

700 g/1½ lb courgettes, trimmed and
  thickly sliced

125 g/4 oz fresh spinach lasagne

2 large eggs

2 tbsp double cream

75 g/3 oz mozzarella cheese, grated

25 g/1 oz pecorino cheese, grated

green salad, to serve

TASTY TIP

This recipe is a simplified version of
ratatouille. If preferred, substitute a
small chopped aubergine and a
chopped red pepper for some of
the courgettes.

1 Preheat the oven to 190°C/375°F/Gas Mark 5, 10 minutes before
cooking. Heat the olive oil in a heavy-based pan, add half the onion
and cook gently for 2–3 minutes. Stir in the tomatoes and wine,
then simmer for 20 minutes, or until a thick consistency is formed.
Add the sugar and season to taste with salt and pepper. Reserve.

2 Meanwhile, melt the butter in another pan, add the remaining
onion, the garlic, mushrooms and courgettes and cook for
10 minutes, or until softened.

3 Spread a little tomato sauce in the base of a lightly oiled, 1.4 litre/
2 ½ pint baking dish. Top with a layer of lasagne and spoon over
half the mushroom and courgette mixture. Repeat the layers,
finishing with a layer of lasagne.

4 Beat the eggs and cream together, then pour over the lasagne. Mix
the mozzarella and pecorino cheeses together then sprinkle on top
of the lasagne. Place in the preheated oven and cook for 20 minutes,
or until golden brown. Serve immediately with a green salad.

Baked Macaroni with Mushrooms & Leeks

INGREDIENTS

Serves 4

2 tbsp olive oil

1 onion, peeled and finely chopped

1 garlic clove, peeled and crushed

2 small leeks, trimmed and chopped

450 g/1 lb assorted wild
  mushrooms, trimmed

50 ml/2 fl oz white wine

75 g/3 oz butter

150 ml/¼ pint crème fraîche or
  whipping cream

salt and freshly ground black pepper

75 g/3 oz fresh white breadcrumbs

350 g/12 oz short cut macaroni

1 tbsp freshly chopped parsley,
  to garnish

HELPFUL HINT

Some wild mushrooms are more tender and cook faster than others. Chestnut, porcini (ceps), portabello, enoki and shiitake would all work well here. If you use chanterelles or oyster mushrooms, sauté them with the leeks for 1 minute only as they are fairly delicate.

1 Preheat the oven to 220°C/425°F/Gas Mark 7, 15 minutes before cooking. Heat 1 tablespoon of the olive oil in a large frying pan, add the onion and garlic and cook for 2 minutes. Add the leeks, mushrooms and 25 g/1 oz of the butter, then cook for 5 minutes. Pour in the white wine, cook for 2 minutes then stir in the crème fraîche or cream. Season to taste with salt and pepper.

2 Meanwhile, bring a large pan of lightly salted water to a rolling boil. Add the macaroni and cook according to the packet instructions, or until 'al dente'.

3 Melt 25 g/1 oz of the butter with the remaining oil in a small frying pan. Add the breadcrumbs and fry until just beginning to turn golden brown. Drain on absorbent kitchen paper.

4 Drain the pasta thoroughly, toss in the remaining butter then tip into a lightly oiled 1.4 litre/2½ pint shallow baking dish. Cover the pasta with the leek and mushroom mixture then sprinkle with the fried breadcrumbs. Bake in the preheated oven for 5–10 minutes, or until golden and crisp. Garnish with chopped parsley and serve.

Index